The Theatrical Event

DAVID COLE

The Theatrical Event

A *Mythos*, A Vocabulary, A Perspective

Wesleyan University Press
Middletown, Connecticut

The publisher gratefully acknowledges the support of the publication
of this book by The Andrew W. Mellon Foundation

Library of Congress Cataloging in Publication Data

Cole, David, 1941—
    The theatrical event.

    Bibliography: p.
    1. Theater. I. Title.
PN2039.C64   792   74-21922
ISBN 0-8195-4078-1

Manufactured in the United States of America
First edition

Contents

Theatre closes a great rift in our lives by enabling us to experience imaginative truth as physical presence. It can do this because a theatre script is not only (like any work of art) a world of subsisting imaginative relations, but also a world that can at any moment become present.

Like a shaman, the actor makes a psychic journey to "another world," that of the script. Like a possessed person, the actor undergoes psychic takeover by "another life," that of the script character. Thus shamanic activity and possession behavior frequently resemble theatre, while contemporary rehearsal and actor-training methods often recall the practices of shamans and possession specialists. In the moment of an actor's passing from shamanic voyager to possessed vehicle, the theatre, as an event, is born.

6 "Interpretation"   140

Contemporary audiences and directors alike are made uncomfortable by the universal images in which theatre deals, and so seek about for ways of refusing them: the narrowing "interpretation," the "concept" production, the imputed "purpose." But since the tendency to deal in such images follows directly from the very nature of theatre, to refuse them is ultimately to refuse theatre itself. The way back from such a refusal lies in recognizing that theatre is an event the significance of which is already given in the kind of event it is.

Introduction

OUR experience of theatre lies in fragments that we have no idea how to reassemble. In fact, we are not even sure what they are the fragments of. We include under the heading "theatre" objects and events that, if they do not positively exclude each other, certainly are not related in any very obvious way. Actors exchanging energy; pages in a book; visual patterns; sequences of spoken words; people coming together to work in the presence of other people who watch—any of these can, at a particular moment, be what we *mean* by theatre; but what do we mean by *theatre*? What is the underlying thing, or event, of which these aspects are the aspects—and how does it come to have such dissimilar aspects? What, for example, has theatre as a group transaction to do with theatre as a visual artifact? Or theatre as a social phenomenon to do with theatre as as aggregate of texts? In what sense can an unstaged script and an unscripted staging be spoken of as belonging to the same activity? Indeed, limiting the question only to scripts: how can a single thing be susceptible of investigation by methods as diverse as Emotion Memory and magazine articles?

To deal with such questions, we do not need a "theory" of theatre, in the sense that one speaks of a theory of wave motion or crystal growth. What we do need is a *perspective* and a *vocabulary*: a *perspective* from which apparently unrelated phenomena can be seen as having the relation which in fact they have; and a *vocabulary* that makes it possible to talk about related phenomena in terms of the thing that relates them. The unity is there; it does not need to be supplied by us. All we have to do is to lift the grid that our categorizing habit of thought has laid over it. All we have to find is a vantage from which the seemingly random points are revealed as lying along one line.

I believe that I have found such a vantage in the concept of theatre as an opportunity to experience imaginative life as physical presence. Everything that figures in theatre can be understood in terms of the role it plays in this process of manifestation. The script is the home or source of the imaginative life to be made present (Chapter 1). The actor is one who seeks out this imaginative life in its home in order to make it present (Chapter 2). The audience are those to whom the imaginative life becomes present (Chapter 3). The scenic means make present those aspects of the imaginative world that the actor himself cannot (Chapter 4). Dramatic language makes present the life of consciousness in that world (Chapter 5). When theatre fails, there has been a refusal of presence, either on the part of the performers or on the part of the spectators or by both (Chapter 6).

In developing and presenting these ideas, I have made extensive use of extra theatrical concepts and terms; however, the fields from which I have borrowed my conceptual tools are none of them the field to which I see this book as making a contribution. Since I should like to avoid arousing expectations that I cannot gratify, let me try to state unequivocally what level of explanation I have aimed at and what levels I have not.

This book is not dramatic criticism. I am concerned with the analysis of particular scripts and productions only insofar as these exemplify a general principle or tendency under discussion.

This book is not an historical or anthropological account of the origins of theatre. I have introduced historical and anthropological material only when I felt it provided a striking confirmation or a useful terminology. The only "origin of theatre" in which I am interested is that which takes place every evening at 8:30.

This book is not an attempt to claim a sacred dimension or religious function for theatre. Religious emotions and ritual practices enter the discussion only as analogies for the emotions and practices that arise in theatre work.

This book is not a psychological explanation of theatre. While that level would be less misleading than the preceding ones, my emphasis is on the total form of the theatrical event and only secondarily on the experience of those caught up in it. As with anthropology, theatre history, and comparative religion, I have borrowed insights from psychology only when such borrowings seemed to me to promise a gain in suggestiveness or clarity.

What, the reader may be wondering, does that leave for the book to be?

There exists (though not to any great extent in the English-speaking countries) a distinguished body of writing on what is sometimes called performance theory. The Symbolists' description of theatre as a working model of the synesthetic *symbole;* the efforts of Craig and Appia to connect dramatic and pictorial values; Stanislavski's redefinition of script exploration as self-exploration; Brecht's correlation of the resources of stage expression with the virtues of Marxian thought process; Artaud's conception of theatre as a multisensory ideogram; Grotowski's account of performance as the performance of a renunciation—all these represent attempts to view the theatrical event from the perspective of a single unifying concept that explains as it unifies.

This is approximately the tradition that I regard myself as working in. But with one important difference. The persons whom I have mentioned wrote with the aim either of defending a theatre style that they practiced or of bringing about a theatre style that they admired. As a result, their theories tend to be fully applicable to no type of theatre but their own. I believe that the perspective I offer, insofar as it applies to any theatrical event, applies to all: to Brecht as much as to Grotowski; to *Peter Pan* as much as to Peter Brook; to what I happen to dislike as much as to what I happen to admire.

If I had to say in one word what I feel this book has to offer, I should say a *mythos* of theatre: an imaginative encompassing of the theatrical event that has as its function not to *be true*, but to *render coherent*. I am throughout more concerned to enable perception than to impart perceptions. I do not regard what I have written as capable of being either proved or refuted. All this book says is: "Try thinking about the theatre *this* way." I am content that it should stand or fall by the consequences of that attempt.

The Theatrical Event

CHAPTER 1

Theatre and the Script

WE live between two kinds of truth, neither of which fully satisfies our criteria of what truth should be like, and each of which seems to exclude the other. *Imaginative truth* satisfies our longing for coherence, but is only an envisioning, cannot *be there*. Whereas the kind of physical reality that *can* be there—let us call it *present truth*—while it meets our demand that truth should be seeable and graspable, lacks the coherence of imaginative form. Imaginative truth and present truth each provide what the other lacks, but only at the expense of lacking what the other provides.

Works of nontheatrical art, while they provide splendid instances of imaginative truth, provide no resolution of this dilemma. It is true that artists—especially poets working in the visionary tradition that begins with the English Romantics, includes the Symbolists, and culminates in Rilke, Valéry, and Yeats—have often made this dilemma their theme. Not vision itself, but how to put moments of vision together with the rest of experience is the perennial concern of visionary poetry: "Fled is that music:—do I wake or sleep?"[1] But not even such a magnificent posing of the problem as *Ode to a Nightingale* brings it any nearer to a solution.

It is, of course, possible to deny that any dilemma exists: one has only to refuse to acknowledge the validity of one or the other of these types of truth. But either of these refusals is fraught with danger.

To refuse imaginative truth is not just to forego "art" or "culture," it is to deny that whole affiliating aspect of consciousness by which alone coherence can begin to characterize our thought. It is to choose a life lived in bondage to unconscious drives and unacknowledged symbolisms. It is to opt for repression.

On the other hand, to refuse present truth in favor of imaginative is not to come forward as the champion of art over fact, but only to make an act of submission to facticity. To assert: "imagination is the only reality" is to concede that only *as* reality can imagination be valued. Such an attitude easily shades into the pathological, as in the case of the schizophrenic who, when asked why she did not take down an etching that bothered her, replied, "If I do, I'll be it"; or another who, when questioned as to the whereabouts of her husband, answered that he was on the wedding picture.[2] But even when no derangement is involved, the need to project imaginings as present betrays a secret prejudice in favor of presence. That they have to be thought of *as present* implies that they are mistrusted *as imaginative*.

As for the possibility of not rejecting either of these kinds of truth, but rather of somehow synthesizing the two, I question for how many of us that can ever be a real possibility. A spectacularly gifted visionary like Wordsworth may have felt able to proclaim:

> How exquisitely the individual Mind
> (And the progressive powers perhaps no less
> Of the whole species) to the external World
> Is fitted:—and how exquisitely, too—
> Theme this but little heard of among men—
> The external World is fitted to the Mind;
> And the creation (by no lower name
> Can it be called) which they with blended might
> Accomplish.[3]

A Rilke may have had moments when

> the external thing itself—tower, mountain, bridge—already possessed the unheard of, unsurpassable intensity of those inner equivalents by means of which it might have been represented. Everywhere appearance and vision came, as it were, together in the object, in every one of them a whole inner world was exhibited.[4]

But most of us, most of the time, are likely to feel, with Sartre, that "the real and the imaginary cannot coexist by their very nature. . . . To prefer the imaginary . . . is not only an escape from the content of the real (poverty, frustrated love, failure of one's enterprise, etc.), but from the form of the real itself, its character of *presence*."[5]

Such would be the extent of the gap in our experience between imagination and presence, if we did not possess in theatre a means of linking them.

Theatre, and theatre alone of human activities, provides an opportunity of experiencing imaginative truth as present truth. In theatre, imaginative events take on for a moment the presentness of physical events; in theatre, physical events take on for a moment the perfection of imaginative form. Especially in the figure of the actor—at once a role-possessed body and an embodied role—imagination and presence come up against each other in a way that allows us to test the strengths of each against the claims of the other.

Theatre is thus an instrumentality by which we are able to *explore experimentally* a dilemma that otherwise we could only *pose conceptually*, and thereby perhaps to advance beyond the impasse which, as we have seen, characterizes this dilemma on the conceptual level.

Theatre, then, is not so much an art as it is an experiment performed on behalf of all the arts. *What has imagination's kind of truth to do with the truth that is present* is a question which any artist might raise, but which only the theatre artist can experiment with. All the arts, to some extent, *make present*; theatre alone *makes presence*. (It is nothing new to observe that the distinctive characteristic of a theatre performance is "presence"; but this is generally misconstrued as referring to the presence of the *actors*. Of course the actors are there—where else should they be?—but what distinguishes theatre from the other arts is that it makes *imaginative truth* present, or rather, makes it presence.)

However, before we can understand the process by which theatre "makes presence," we must ask what it is about the imaginative structures with which theatre deals that enables them to *become* present in a way that poems and novels cannot. This amounts to asking for a definition of a script.

"Script" is not one of those critical terms we are accustomed to think of as giving us trouble. If I refer to "the script of *East Lynne*," everyone knows I mean the little booklet in which are set down the words that, when spoken aloud by actors with appropriate gestures and movements, constitute a performance of *East Lynne*. And if it should be objected that not all performances take their origin from words set down to be spoken, the definition easily can—and certainly should—be broadened to include, say, the instructions for a sound-and-movement exercise or the conventions of a buck-and-wing dance. If, then, we declare a script to be *any more or less detailed set of instructions for putting on a performance, whether written by a playwright, imparted by a director, or evolved by a group of actors from their rehearsal probings*, we would seem to have given a definition inclusive of virtually everything and offensive to practically no one.

The trouble arises when we try to state the role of each participant in theatre in terms of a relation to the "script," so defined. This ought to be simple enough, since each of them must stand in some relation to it. But when we have got through stating all the relations, it no longer seems as if there could be a single thing capable of having all these different relations taken toward it. For the actors the script is an occasion for certain processes of personal and interpersonal exploration. For the director it is a set of guidelines for constructing a stage action. For the designer it is a coding in nonvisual terms of certain visual motifs. For the critic or teacher it is a kind of order which he must try to talk about in terms of another kind of order. For an audience it is the aura of calculation that hangs over a living event. Even the author (assuming for a moment that we are talking about a written play) may regard his creation in any number of different ways: as a verbal artifact; as an event in which others merely take their place (or conversely, as a mere catalyst of creativity in others); as a sequence of manipulations to be performed upon an audience; as a depiction.

But what must the script itself be in order for so many different relations to it to be possible? The answer to this question is crucial to understanding how theatre is able to make presence. A script is—and theatre can make presence because the form of imaginative life in which it deals is—what writers on comparative religion call an *illud tempus*.

Most religions possess the concept of an *illud tempus*, a time of origins, the period of Creation and just after, when gods walked the earth, men visited the sky, and the great archetypal events of myth—war in heaven, battles with monsters, the Quest, the Flood, the Fall—took place. *Genesis*, *The Epic of Gilgamesh*, and Greek mythology are familiar portrayals of the world *in illo tempore*, "in those days."

The remarkable thing about the *illud tempus* is that whereas one might suppose it, of all eras, to have vanished irretrievably, it in fact can—unlike the merely historical periods which follow it—be made present again at any moment, by the performance of a ritual:

> Every ritual has the character of happening *now*, at this very moment. The time of the event that the ritual commemorates or re-enacts is made *present*, "re-presented" so to speak, however far back it may have been in ordinary reckoning. Christ's passion, death and resurrection are not simply *remembered*

during the services of Holy Week; they really happen *then* before the eyes of the faithful.[6]

In a word, the *illud tempus* is not so much *when it first oc-curred* as *where it is always happening*. And further, since what is always happening is ever-accessible, the *illud tempus* has the potential to be, at any moment, among us.

Every work of art proposes to be a self-contained imagi-native universe, and therefore every work of art possesses *one* of the two characteristics of an *illud tempus*: that of being the place where the original events are always happening and the original figures are always to be found. The words of the Father in Pirandello's *Six Characters in Search of an Author*:

> Our reality doesn't change: it can't change! It can't be other than what it is, because it is already fixed for ever. It's terri-ble. Ours is an immutable reality which should make you shudder when you approach us.[7]

are something any god or hero of the *illud tempus*, suddenly granted consciousness of himself *as* an inhabitant of the *illud tempus*, might say. They are also, of course, something any figure in a novel or painting might say, if suddenly granted consciousness of himself as a figure in that novel or painting. But of all the kinds of beings who might speak Pirandello's words, only the theatre character can come before us to do so clad in that very flesh and blood which, as the speech empha-sizes, is so different a way of being alive from his own.

And so, while every work of art possesses one of the two distinguishing characteristics of an *illud tempus*—that of being a universe of eternally subsisting relations—only a theatre script possesses the other qualification as well: the potential to be present.

There is no question about *who* must be the one to actu-alize this potential: while in a sense it is the task of everyone who works in the theatre, it is first and foremost the job of the actor. But *what methods* are there by which an actor can hope to represent a script *illud tempus*? Here it helps to consider the related, though by no means identical, question: what methods are there of representing THE *illud tempus*— the world of archetypal myth itself, to which any particular script *illud tempus* offers itself as rival and alternative?

The primitive knows two ways of making the *illud tempus* present again: in rituals (as was noted above) and in dreams. We may have our doubts about the rituals, but all the findings of modern analytic psychology confirm the primitive's belief that "it is in dreams that the pure sacred life is entered and direct relations with the gods, spirits and ancestral souls are re-established. It is always in dreams that historical time is abolished and the mythical time regained."[8] The Australian aborigines have a word for the *illud tempus* that means "the dream time."[9] In this usage they anticipate the astounding discovery of Jung that the great events of the *illud tempus*—creation, divine warfare, visits to the underworld, and the like—are re-enacted nightly in the dreams of each of us.[10]

As an instance of how archetypal events formerly *presented* in rituals continue to be "*presented*" in dreams, compare the two following accounts—the first of an ancient Babylonian ritual, the second of a contemporary child's dream:

> At Babylon during the last days of the year that was ending and the first days of the New Year, the *Poem of Creation*, the *Enuma elish*, was solemnly recited. This ritual recitation reactualized the combat between Marduk and the marine monster Tiamat, a combat that took place *ab origine* and put an end to chaos by the final victory of the god. This commemoration of the Creation was in fact a reactualization of the cosmogonic act. [A mimed] battle *repeated the passage from chaos to cosmos*, actualized the cosmogony. The mythical event became *present* once again.[11]

> "Once in a dream I saw an animal that had lots of horns. It spiked up other little animals with them. It wriggled like a snake and that was how it lived. Then a blue fog came out of

all the four corners, and it stopped eating. Then God came, but there were really four gods in the four corners. Then the animal died, and all the animals it had eaten came out alive again."[12]

One need not be a worshipper of Marduk to recognize that he is once again triumphing over his old foe Tiamat in the dream of the twentieth-century child.

Dreams, of course, are not a self-contained area of experience; they are the product and reflection of our total mental life. Hence, the real significance of our having located *illud tempus* figures (what Freud called "archaic remnants" and Jung, more appreciatively, "eternal archetypes") in our dreams is that we have thereby identified the *illud tempus* with our psychic interior:

> There is a primordial kinship between the great traditional mythologies . . . and the archetypes . . . which have condensed into "individual mythologies" in the individual human psyche. Who can say when the two first met? For the divine images of the great mythologies are nothing other than projected intrapsychic factors, nothing other than personified archetypal powers, in which human existence rises to the grandeur of the type and is concretized.[13]

So that, returning to the question of what means we possess of making the *illud tempus* (THE *illud tempus*) present, it would seem that the first step must be: exploration of our own minds in search of those "intrapsychic factors" which correspond to its events and personages.

THE *illud tempus* of myth and dream is not, of course, identifiable with any one particular script *illud tempus*, since the very aim of script-making is to create *alternative* worlds of relations. Nonetheless, the preceding discussion suggests that the actor's first step in *pre*senting a script *illud tempus* must likewise be a journey inward in search of those components of his own psychic life that coincide with the figures and events of the script *illud tempus*.

Interior journeys in search of psychic components that correspond to external realities are the specialty of a class of religious practitioners called "shamans." The methods of shamanism therefore shed considerable light on the work of the actor (especially the work of the actor in rehearsal); and it is to them that we now turn.

CHAPTER 2

The Actor

GIVEN the work of Frazer, Cornford, Murray, Gaster, and, most recently, O. B. Hardison, it is nothing new to suggest that there are parallels of structure and intent between theatre performances and rituals. But it is generally the wrong *kind* of ritual which is emphasized in such comparisons.

Any ritual involves a transaction with figures or forces of the *illud tempus*. But whereas some rituals are content to leave the figure or force back in the *illud tempus* while attempting to beseech or compel his aid toward some desired end, there are other rituals where the end desired is, precisely, the presence of the *illud tempus*. I shall call these latter, "*pre*senting rituals."

Hitherto, it has been mainly the former type of ritual that has been seen as comprising the analogy with, and perhaps even the origin of, theatre. This is not surprising. Rituals of the first sort usually make extensive use of symbolic enactment, either as a means of directly achieving their result through sympathetic magic (one moistens the ground to bring on a rainstorm) or as a way of showing the god what result is desired (one moistens the ground to demonstrate one's need of rain). And symbolic enactment can easily be seen as having close affinities with mimesis, which—or so we have become used to thinking—is the very essence of theatre.

Now of course this reasoning could be attacked on the grounds that a ritual observance which aims at making something happen is a very different thing from mimesis, which merely depicts something as happening. But even allowing that symbolic ritual is closely related to mimesis, the real question is how closely related mimesis is to theatre. We have found theatre to be concerned with presence. Mimesis, on the other hand, implies absence: that which is being imitated is "elsewhere"; the imitation is "here." But this is precisely the tidy distinction between imagined and present which, as we saw in Chapter 1, theatre exists to challenge. It would be surprising if the ritual that turned out to have the most to do with theatre should be one that takes this distinction complacently for granted.

No, mimesis is not a major aspect of theatre—not, at any rate, considered as a resource or method; considered as a *subject matter*, mimesis has, as we shall see in Chapter 6,[1] central importance for theatre. And it is to other kinds of ritual than those with affinities to mimesis that we must turn for analogies with, and perhaps (though this does not concern us as much) for the historical origins of, theatre—namely, to what I earlier called "*pre*senting rituals," because through them, men are enabled to "know the presence" of the *illud tempus*.

There are two senses in which it is possible to know the presence of the *illud tempus*, and to each of these corresponds a different type of *pre*senting ritual. Either men can seek to make themselves present in the *illud tempus*, or men can seek to make the *illud tempus* present among them. *Pre*senting rituals that attempt the former kind of presence ("we go there") have the character of spiritual ascents, explorations that lead upward from our world to the *illud tempus*. *Pre*senting rituals that attempt the latter kind of presence ("they come here") bring about descents of *illud tempus* personages into our midst, and with us as their vehicles—that is, bring about divine possession. Each of these rituals requires a brave and knowledgeable practitioner. The former, "we go there," ritual is the specialty of the shaman, the psychic voyager to the world of the gods. The latter, "they come here," ritual is the province of the hungan,° the human being whose presence becomes, through possession, a god's presence.

Both the shaman's voyage and the hungan's possession are, for the person involved, inner experiences. Yet they are inner experiences undertaken on a public behalf. The shaman enacts his society's longing to go among the gods. He is, if you will, their "envoy" to the *illud tempus*. The hungan enacts his society's longing to bring the gods here among us. He, too, is a kind of envoy—an envoy sent by the *illud tempus* to us.

What becomes of all these definitions and distinctions if we take, as in Chapter 1, the *illud tempus* to be that of a theatre script?

The shaman who makes himself present in the *illud tempus* of a theatre script and the hungan by whom some aspect of that "script" *illud tempus* makes itself present among us are, in each case, the actor. Or to put it more clearly: the actor's work has both a shamanic and a hunganic aspect. In that he draws near—through study, psychophysical exercises, and rehearsal work—to the *illud tempus* of the script, he is like a shaman. In that he becomes possessed by the life of one of the inhabitants of that *illud tempus*, he is like a hungan. For the actor, as for actual shamans and hungans, the "journeying toward" and the "possession by" are inner experiences; but also as with actual shamans and hungans, these inner experiences serve a public function. The actor-as-shaman is the audience's envoy to the *illud tempus* of the script: he draws near that the audience may draw near. The

---

°*Hungan* is the Haitian term for the priest of a possession cult. I use it to mean a person of any nationality who seeks possession as a blessed state of nearness to the gods, rather than flees it as a demonic affliction—a distinction which is discussed below, pp. 33-34, 43-45.

actor-as-hungan is the script's envoy to the audience: he consents to possession so that the audience may have figures from the script *illud tempus* present in the flesh.

In the pages that follow I shall develop each of these analogies in detail, but even at this early stage it is important to recognize the paradox that seems to arise from allowing both analogies at once. We have seen that shamanism and hunganism are diametrically opposite modes of contact with the *illud tempus*. As Luc de Heusch puts it: "Possession is opposed to shamanism in this respect: that whereas shamanism is a movement upward of man toward the gods, ascensional in both technique and doctrine, possession is a movement downward on the part of the gods, an incarnation."[2] And yet it is my contention that the work of the actor has both a shamanic and a hunganic aspect. How can this be?

The question can be fully answered only after a careful examination of each role has revealed a basis for continuity between them. But I shall anticipate my conclusions so far as to suggest that for the actor, shamanism and hunganism are not alternative modes of encountering the (script) *illud tempus*, but rather the two successive phases of his encounter with it. In the manner of a shaman, he opens a "way out" toward the *illud tempus*, and then, in the manner of a hungan, he *himself becomes* the "way back" of the *illud tempus* toward us.

I call this reversal in which the actor goes from shaman to hungan—from masterful explorer to mastered vehicle—the "rounding." The rounding is the defining characteristic of theatrical performance. It is in the moment of the rounding that the theatre, as an event, is born.

There is one matter of terminology to be cleared up before we plunge into the analysis that will give substance to these generalizations. In the following discussion and henceforth, I use the word "Image," with a capital *i*, to mean, roughly, an inhabitant or personage of a script *illud tempus*.

Why not simply say "character" or "role"? For two reasons. First, because I wish to emphasize that the beings whom actors (and through them, audiences) encounter are numinous dwellers in an eternal imaginative *illud tempus*, not just an assortment of persons who happen to be imaginary. To call such beings "Images" at once stresses their otherness (we need the actor-as-shaman to approach them) and their insubstantiality (they need the actor-as-hungan to be present). And the term has the further advantage of describing how such beings subsist in the individual and communal mind, namely, as "Images" from our reading and theatre-going.

My second reason for the choice of the term "Image" follows from my definition of a theatre script in Chapter 1. If "theatre script" is to mean, not just the text of a play, but any set of instructions for performance, a term of comparable breadth must be found for the human figures involved. "Character" conjures up figures on the order of Goneril or John Gabriel Borkman—and indeed, Goneril and Borkman are "Images" in my sense of the word: imaginative beings whom actors seek to "be present to" and to make present. But I need a word that can equally well describe that which a hula dancer or a *commedia* clown or a participant in a mirror-exercise is trying to be present to and to make present. In these cases, "character" is too suggestive of an individual-ized personality, while "role" implies a set of problems rather than a human figure. I therefore choose "Image" as being free of most of the wrong connotations and suggestive in several of the right directions. I shall, however, sometimes speak of "roles" and "characters" when there is no danger of a misunderstanding.

Shamanism is a religious practice found all over the world from Africa to the Arctic, from South America to Polynesia. In some cultures it is the dominant religious mode; in others it exists side by side with more conventional forms of worship.

This diversity has resulted in some confusion as to what is and is not distinctively shamanic. The shaman has been characterized as everything from an herbalist to a juggler, but most often as a medicine man, magician, or priest.[3] Of these, none is wholly accurate; but "priest" is wholly misleading. The priest remains an outsider to the supernatural world he manipulates; the shaman directly experiences the supernatural.[4] Priestly rituals often have the character of a reenactment—a mimesis—of a journey to the other world;[5] shamans are believed to be able to make that journey.

Nor will "magician" or "medicine man" suffice to characterize the shaman. While shamans often function as magicians and medicine men, it is quite possible to be a magician or medicine man without being a shaman.

What is it, then, that shamans can do that other religious practitioners cannot? The shaman, writes Eliade, "specializes in a trance during which his soul is believed to leave his body and ascend to the sky or descend to the underworld."[6] In other words, the shaman visits the *illud tempus*.

For the shaman himself, of course, this is an intensely inner experience, a visionary "trip." But I shall for the moment confine myself to considering the public function of this inner experience.

Visiting the *illud tempus*, it is widely believed, was once a universal human privilege.[7] It is, incidentally, this belief that explains why men should ever have begun regarding what is in fact a realm of eternally present archetypes as an historically earliest period. If the *illud tempus* was once accessible to man, this could only have been in the very earliest times, for no subsequent generation has had such access. In those days, "communication between heaven and earth was possible"; but subsequently, "in consequence of a certain event or a ritual fault, the communication was broken off."[8]

The immense value of a shaman to his society lies in the fact that in his trance-journeys he restores this once universal access. Shamans "periodically undertake the ecstatic journey to the sky; by doing so, they in a manner abolish the present fallen state of the universe and humanity and re-establish the primordial situation, when heaven was easily accessible to all men.">[9] This is no idle feat of spiritual virtuosity; by means of it, the shaman's tribesmen acquire influence and representation in the *illud tempus*. For the shaman does not simply make the journey we all dream of making; he makes it on our behalf, as our envoy. The shaman goes to the gods "to present the wishes of the community."[10]

In all this there is a close parallel with the work of the actor. To grasp it, we have only to understand the *illud tempus* in question as being a theatre script, and the "community," on whose behalf the journey there is undertaken, as being the theatre public (by which I mean not just those in the audience on a given night, but all those in the society of which the actor is a member who desire contact with that script). Like the shaman, the actor makes the journey to the (script) *illud tempus*. Like the shaman, he goes there on behalf of those who have heard accounts (i. e., have read or heard about the script), but cannot go there themselves. Like the shaman, he conveys to this *illud tempus* (or more exactly, to the particular inhabitant of it he has been entrusted with contacting) the "wishes of the community," that is, the desire of every theatre-goer for a more immediate knowledge of the script *illud tempus* than can be had from the script. Also like the shaman, the actor experiences his journey to the *illud tempus* as psychic and inward; but it is similarities of public role we are concerned with at the moment.

The suggestion that the actor is a kind of shaman gains in plausibility from the fact that, in most cultures, the shaman is a kind of actor.

Many witnesses have been struck by the theatrical nature of the séances in which a shaman sends his spirit forth to the *illud tempus*.[11] The mere fact that these séances are usually performed in public, for onlookers—an unusual setting for ecstatic experience—gives them the aura of a performance situation. But the resemblances go far beyond that. In fact, it is difficult to think of a single aspect of theatre that cannot also be an aspect of shamanic "performance."

The most basic respect in which these events resemble theatre is the considerable amount of mimed action and spoken dialogue they contain. The shaman laboriously mimes the ascent or descent to the other world which his soul is at that moment making (*Figure 1*). This may involve, if it is an ascent, his climbing a mountain or flying like a bird; or, if it is a descent, his opening the earth and passing through it, crossing a narrow bridge, or swimming to the bottom of the sea.[12] Once arrived in the other world, he uses mime to transmit back to his onlookers the adventures he is, psychically, having there: battles against divine animals or demons, social contact with gods.[13] The latter often gives rise to dialogues, in which the shaman speaks for both himself and the deity.[14] The shaman must be something of an expert in vocal characterization, for in the course of one of these dialogues he may be called upon to produce everything from the sound of a horse drinking to the hiccups of a god.[15] In addition to mime and dialogue, the shaman may draw on such incidental performance skills as ventriloquism[16] and puppetry[17] to help render his adventures in the other world.

Shamanic performance also has a scenic dimension that allies it with theatre. The shaman employs costumes, properties, music, even primitive lighting effects and scene-changes. Shamans' costumes range from animal suits to stylized representations of the human skeleton, and often display elaborate color symbolism.[18] A shaman's properties can include such diverse items as baskets of paper flowers, brooms, and flags.[19] Music is provided both by accompanying drummers and by the shaman himself, who may play upon a trumpetlike or violinlike instrument, or simply shake rattles and bells. (Seed pods and bells are sometimes sewn right into his costume, making him a virtual one-man band.)[20] Brilliant lamps, sinking hearth-fires, lighted candles, gun flashes, and sparking brands tossed aloft into the air are among the lighting effects employed in shamanic perfor-

Figure 1: A Bornean shaman mimes his journey to the *illud tempus*. The symbolic constructions, at the center and the right, around which he dances gives a scenic dimension to the ceremony. *Photograph by J. Dournes; courtesy of Musée de l'Homme, Paris.*

mance.[21] Set-changes are accomplished by the rearrangement of objects in the room to correspond to each new site the shaman visits in his "wanderings."[22]

Two sure signs of dramatic impulse in any ritual are the interpolation of comic episodes and the appearance of additional actors. Both these tendencies are in evidence in shamanic séances. For example, Siberian shamans mime such comic scenes as the offering of tobacco to a bird.[23] And in Koniag and Toba séances, large segments of the audience join in the song and dance, sometimes taking the performance out of the shaman's hands.[24]

Finally in this connection, it is interesting to note what personality traits are thought, in many cultures, to mark one as a potential shaman: "Frequent fainting-fits, excitable and sensitive disposition, taciturnity, moroseness, love of solitude and other symptoms of a susceptible nervous system."[25] This profile closely corresponds to our own notion of the "star" temperament as sensitive, volatile, and moody.

But it is not enough to show that shamanism is, in some peripheral respects, theatrical. We want to know whether acting is, in any essential respect, shamanic. We have already seen that in his public role, as a community's envoy to an *illud tempus*, the actor performs a function distinctly parallel to that of the shaman. We must now go on to enquire whether the parallel extends to the inner experience of each as he goes about fulfilling this public role.

Primitive peoples believe the *illud tempus* to be an actual historical period and not merely, as in our view, a constellation of mental archetypes. Nonetheless, for them, too, the *illud tempus* is within—not, as for us, *only* within, but *also* within.[26] Consequently, any voyage there is going to have to be pursued through outer and inner space simultaneously, through the cosmos and through the mind.

From the point of view of the community that sends him, the space through which the shaman journeys is cosmological. Shamans are thought of as "going up to the sky" via a "central opening," which they penetrate by means of a ladder, rope, bridge, or mountain—all objects which figure prominently in shamanic rite and imagery.[27]

But for the shaman himself, whose means of "ascent" is ecstasy, not rockets, the space traversed is interior: "What for the rest of the community remains a cosmological ideogram, for the shamans . . . becomes a mystical itinerary."[28] And the means of traversing it (shamanism and modern psychology are at one on this point) is the dream:

> It is in dreams that the pure sacred life is entered and direct relations with the gods, spirits and ancestral souls are re-established. It is always in dreams that historical time is abolished and the mythical time regained.[29]
>
> The pattern of shamanism is primarily the dream journey to the house of the supernatural being.[30]

The *illud tempus* which the actor seeks is likewise at once without and within; and for him, too, the "space" through which he must travel to get there is both external and inner. Considered in his public role—as a community's envoy to a script—the actor makes a journey between two points external to himself: from his audience's mental life to the script *illud tempus*. But the actor himself experiences this journey as inward, as what Grotowski calls a "self-penetration."[31] For the actor as for the shaman, an inward journey is the sole means by which a journey can be performed on behalf of others. The shaman can explore the archetypal world of the *illud tempus* only by seeking those archetypes in his own fantasies, memories, and dreams. The actor can explore an *illud tempus* which is the work of another man's imagination only by exploring his own psyche for answering impulses, shared fantasies, common symbolisms: "In the beginning his understanding of the inner significance of a play is necessarily too general. Usually he will not get to the bottom of it until he has thoroughly studied it by following the steps the author took when he first wrote it."[32] The way to the Image lies through the self. In searching for the life of a role, it is one's own life one searches.

There is, then, this general similarity between the experience of the actor and that of the shaman: each in some sense makes a journey to his psychic interior. But what lends interest to the general similarity are the many specific parallels between shamanism and acting that it makes visible.

Many of these similarities come to light in the form of metaphors used by actors and acting teachers to describe the imaginative process of investigating a role. Time and again in the writings of Stanislavski and others we find the actor's approach to his Image described in terms that strongly suggest the shaman's approach to his god. Here, as in so many areas of modern life, the archaic original of an activity shows through the language used in, and of, that activity.

Are we, however, justified in drawing conclusions about a primarily nonverbal activity from primarily verbal evidence? In the first place, as the New Critics and psychoanalysts have each in their own way taught us, there is no surer indicator of the character of a person's inner experience than the metaphors he is driven to use to describe it. Even when, as in some of the examples we shall consider, a statement seems little more than bad rhetoric, there still remains the question: Why this *particular* bad rhetoric?

Another point to bear in mind is that in rehearsals and acting classes, metaphors are *for use*. That is to say, they are flung out by the director or teacher for the sake of what they set going in the actors' minds—for example: "The body movement must be sharp and strong like the bows of a ship cleaving a huge wave";[33] "See it with your elbow!"[34] "See how much of this room you can fill with yourself."[35] If the kinds of metaphors that function best for this purpose are those most reminiscent of shamanic practices, that is strong evidence of a similarity between the mental processes of actor and shaman.

Of course not all approaches to acting are shamanic to the same degree. Stanislavski's is most particularly so, and the greater part of my examples will therefore be drawn from his writings. But all acting methods are in touch with shamanism to some extent, and I shall have occasion to note shamanic elements in approaches to acting as different from Stanislavski's—and from each other—as those of Gordon Craig, Max Reinhardt, Jerzy Grotowski, Viola Spolin, and Living Theatre member Steve Ben Israel.

The fundamental shamanic experience is a search in a dream. With that in mind, consider the metaphors Stanislavski uses in each of the following passages to suggest the actor's experience of approach to the Image:

> Can you picture to yourself what our emotion memory is really like? Imagine a number of houses, with many rooms in each house, in each room innumerable cupboards, shelves, boxes, and somewhere, in one of them, a tiny bead. It is easy enough to find the right house, room, cupboard, and shelf. But it is more difficult to find the right box. And where is the sharp eye that will find that tiny bead that rolled out today, glittered for a moment, and then disappeared from sight—only luck will ever find it again.
> That is what it is like in the archives of your memory.[36]

> I realize that I cannot achieve this sense of nearness, really feel it, by digging in the text of the play while sitting at my desk . . .
> How can I accomplish this shift? It . . . is done with the help of imagination—but this time imagination plays an active rather than a passive role.
> You can be the observer of your dream, but you can also take an active part in it—that is you can find yourself mentally in the center of circumstances and conditions, a way of life, furnishings, objects, and so forth, which you have imagined. You no longer see yourself as an outside onlooker, but you see what surrounds you. In time, when this feeling of "being" is reinforced, you can become the main active personality in the surrounding circumstances of your dream; you can begin, mentally, to act.[37]

The first passage implies that preparation of a role is a dream-like search; the second, that it is a dream of searching. Whichever way the emphasis tilts, the net effect of such metaphors is to affirm an affinity between the psychic experiences of shamanizing and acting.

It will be recalled that Eliade's basic definition of shamanism[38] stressed three elements:

(1) A state of trance
(2) A mental journey to the *illud tempus* conceived of as a heaven
(3) A mental journey to the *illud tempus* conceived of as an underworld

Each of these motifs is present in actors' and acting teachers' characteristic ways of talking and thinking about their art.

Take first the motif of trance, "a condition of dissociation, characterized by the lack of voluntary movement, and frequently by automatism in act and thought."[39] It is hard to think of two more opposed conceptions of the actor than those of Gordon Craig (the actor as dehumanized puppet) and Grotowski (the actor as fully humanized "saint"). Yet these two men, who agree on little else, agree on the necessity of the actor's being in a state of trance, which Craig defines as "a death-like beauty . . . exhaling a living spirit,"[40] and Grotowski, as the ability "to refrain from doing something . . . to concentrate in a particular theatrical way."[41] "Trance" is not a word that Stanislavski is partial to; however, his account of "Kostya's sea voyage," discussed below in connection with the shaman's journey to the underworld, clearly represents the actor's highest creative state as a kind of trance.[42]

Human beings tend to think of the gods as, in some sense, "above." It is therefore not surprising that the shaman's journey to the gods is often conceptualized as an ascent. The shaman is often imagined as climbing up to the gods by a rope, either one let down from heaven[43] or one sent up from earth (here doubtless we have the origin of the "Indian rope trick").[44] The Niassans of Sumatra think of their shamans as travelling to the sky in an eagle-drawn boat.[45] Everywhere ladders and stairs figure prominently in the iconography of the shamanic voyage.[46]

Ascent and flight are likewise common metaphors, in several schools of acting, for the actor's approach to his Image. One of the main aids Stanislavski offers the actor is the "magic if":[47]

> "At this point, I am not so much interested in the action itself as in the approach to it. That is why I suggest that you, Paul, are living the life of a tree."
> "Good," said Paul with decision. "I am an age-old oak! However, even though I have said it, I don't really believe it."
> "In that case," suggested the Director, "why don't you say to yourself: 'I am I; but *if* I were an old oak, set in certain surrounding conditions, what would I do?'"[48]

The "magic if" is intended at once to liberate the actor's imagination from a debilitating sense of sham ("I don't really believe it"), and to stimulate the imagination which it thus liberates. The metaphor in which Stanislavski describes the results of this valuable technique is therefore significant: "*If* acts as a lever to lift us out of the world of actuality into the realm of imagination."[49] The "magic if" is seen as making possible a shamanic ascent ("lifts us") from the "world of actuality" to the *illud tempus* ("realm of imagination").

Max Reinhardt is a director better known for his exploration of the physical stage than for his insights into the psychology of acting. This fact makes it all the more striking that his account of the actor's work is couched in an imagery of shamanic flight:

> We can telegraph and telephone and wire pictures across the ocean; we can fly over it. But the way to the human being next us is still as far as to the stars. The actor takes us on this way. With the light of the poet he climbs the unexplored peaks of the human soul, his own soul, in order to transform it secretly there and to return with his hands, eyes and voice full of wonders.[50]

The actor-shaman is here described as making an ascensional journey ("to the stars," "climbs the unexplored peaks") on behalf of his audience ("takes us on this way") so that he may bring them back the presence ("return with his hands, eyes, and voice full of wonders") of an *illud tempus* at once without and within ("the human soul, his own soul").

A member of the Living Theatre, suddenly in touch with an Image he had been reaching for in an exercise, describes the moment this way: "So in my own experience, I waited for that point and all of a sudden, it was, like, Oh my God. When that happened, I just flew."[51] For actors as close to actual religious experience as the Becks' troupe, "Oh my God" is more than an expletive and "flew" more than an overstatement. We have here something between the description of an acting experience in shamanic metaphor and the description of an actual shamanic experience of flight to the gods.

Inevitably, the belief that shamans can fly has led to their being associated with, and depicted as, birds. Shamanic costume often imitates or incorporates parts of birds, in some cases becoming a complete bird-outfit.[52] In central Asia shamans were formerly believed to be able to turn themselves into birds.[53] (There is perhaps a late literary survival of this symbolism in such poems as Shelley's *To a Skylark* and Keats's *Ode to a Nightingale*, in which the human speaker, by fusing imaginatively with a bird, becomes capable of journeys to transcendental realms.)

These facts provide a significant context in which to interpret the following acting exercise of Grotowski's:

Flight
1. Squatting on the heels in a curled up position, hop and sway like a bird ready to take flight. The hands help the movement as wings.
2. Still hopping, raise yourself into an upright position, while the hands flap like wings in an effort to lift the body.[54]

Such an exercise seems designed to bring home to the actor his function as shamanic flier to the *illud tempus*. And when

Grotowski goes on to recommend that the actor "recall to mind the flying sensation one experiences in dreams and spontaneously recreate this form of flight,"[55] he is specifically associating the actor's inward quest for the Image with the shamanic motifs of dream-quest and flight. Here again, confirmation from a surprising quarter is provided by Max Reinhardt:

> These [primitive man's efforts at acting] were the first attempts *to fly above* his narrow material existence. The possibilities inherent in him but not brought to full growth by his life thus *unfolded their shadowy wings* and *carried him far over* his knowledge and *away into the heart of a strange experience*. He discovered all the delights of transformation, all the ecstasy of passion, all the illusive *life of dreams*.[56] [italics mine]

Another point to note in this connection is the almost ubiquitous use, in actor-training classes, of exercises in which the student is instructed to turn himself into an animal.[57] These exercises, too, betray the shamanic nature of acting. The shaman is generally believed capable of transforming himself into an animal, and in his "performances" often mimes doing so.[58] Though not specifically ascensional in their symbolism, such transformations have the same meaning—and establish the same connection between shamanism and acting —as does the depiction of the shaman as a bird. For like birds, animals are commonly regarded as guides to the other world,[59] and so constitute natural roles for shamans and actors equally, those expert voyagers to their respective *illa tempora*.

The other world contains terrifying as well as blessed regions, and when the shaman seeks these out, his journey is often imagined as a descent to the underworld:

> The [Altaic] shaman makes a vertical descent down the seven successive "levels," or subterranean regions, called *pudak*, "obstacles." He is accompanied by his ancestors and his helping spirits. As each obstacle is passed, he sees

a new subterranean epiphany; the word *black* recurs in almost every verse. At the second "obstacle" he apparently hears metallic sounds; at the fifth, waves and the wind whistling; finally, at the seventh, where the nine subterranean rivers have their mouths, he sees Erlik Khan's palace, built of stone and black clay and defended in every direction. The shaman utters a long prayer to Erlik . . . then he returns to the yurt and tells the audience the results of his journey.[60]

A similar descent is attributed to the actor in the following simile of Stanislavski's:

The conscious levels of a play or part are like the levels and strata of the earth, sand, clay, rocks and so forth, which go to form the earth's crust. As the levels go deeper down into one's soul they become increasingly unconscious, and down in the very depths, in the core of the earth where you find molten lava and fire, invisible human instincts and passions are raging.[61]

Note that the successive levels are at once those of a play (or part) and those of the actor's own consciousness. As we have seen, the shaman-actor's penetration of the script *illud tempus* is simultaneously a penetration of his self.

Among many peoples, especially maritime peoples, the underworld is thought to be situated in the depths of the sea, and the rites connected with the shaman's visits there involve a symbolism of diving and immersion.[62] I mention this fact because without it, the most shamanic passage in all of Stanislavski's writings might not be recognizable as such. The first-year acting student Kostya is playing, for the *n*th time, an exercise in which a bank clerk discovers that his half-witted brother-in-law has flung into the fire a huge sum of money for which he, the bank clerk, is responsible. Kostya is having no luck reaching his Image—he is tired of journeys to this particular *illud tempus*—when all of a sudden "the unexpected happened. I found myself in an unfamiliar room, one I had not been in before. There was an aged couple, my wife's parents. This unprepared for circumstance affected and stirred me."[63] Whereupon Kostya is propelled on a truly shamanic descent into the "*ocean of his subconscious*," as the teacher, Tortsov, calls it (I italicize the phrases in which Tortsov describes Kostya's experience in terms of a shamanic immersion descent):

> Out of the corner of my ear I heard Tortsov make some approving comment and explain to the students that this was the right approach to the subconscious. But I no longer paid any attention to encouragement. I did not need it because I was really living on the stage and could do anything I chose.
>
> Evidently the Director, having achieved his pedagogic purpose was ready to interrupt me but I was eager to cling to my point and I went right on.
>
> "Oh, I see," said he to the others. "*This is a big wave.*" Nor was I satisfied. I wanted to complicate my situation further and enhance my emotions. So I added a new circumstance: a substantial defalcation in my accounts. In admitting that possibility I said to myself: What would I do? At the very thought my heart was in my mouth.
>
> "*The water is up to his waist now,*" commented Tortsov.
>
> "What can I do?" I said excitedly, "I must get back to the office!" I rushed toward the vestibule. Then I remembered that the office was closed, so I came back and paced up and down trying to gather my thoughts. I finally sat down in a dark corner to think things out.
>
> I could see, in my mind's eye, some severe persons going over the books and counting the funds. They questioned me but I did not know how to answer. An obstinate kind of despair kept me from making a clean breast.
>
> Then they wrote out a resolution, fatal to my career. They stood around in groups, whispering. I stood to one side, an outcast. Then an examination, trial, dismissal, confiscation of property, loss of home.
>
> "*He is out in the ocean of the subconscious now,*" said the Director. Then he leaned over the footlights and said softly to me: "Don't hurry, go through to the very end."
>
> He turned to the other students again and pointed out that, although I was motionless, you could feel the storm of emotions inside of me.

I heard all these remarks, but they did not interfere with my life on the stage, or draw me away from it. At this point my head was swimming with excitement because my part and my own life were so intermingled that they seemed to merge. I had no idea where one began or the other left off. My hand ceased wrapping the string around my fingers and I became inert.

"*That is the very depth of the ocean*," explained Tortsov.[64]

What significance is there in the fact that "ascent" and "descent" can equally well be used as metaphors for the actor's (or shaman's) experience? The ambivalent symbolism points up an ambivalence in the experiences themselves, the potential they contain for self-loss as well as self-penetration,[65] the great emotional range they demand of those who would embark on them.

A final instance of the ties between acting and shamanism can be observed in an approach to acting seemingly far removed from shamanism. Viola Spolin, the great apostle of "improvisation for the theatre," denies that an actor will find anything he can use on the stage in the depths of his psyche. "Subjective emotion carried to the stage," she claims, "is not communication."[66] That would seem to leave no place for anything resembling shamanic methods. However, such methods are not absent from Spolin's arsenal:

The Relaxed Rehearsal

. . . The actors lie on the floor, shut their eyes, and breathe slowly with strong accent on the exhale. The director walks around from time to time, lifting a foot or a hand to make sure muscular release is complete.

The actors then go through the lines of the play as they lie there with their eyes closed. They are to concentrate on visualizing the stage . . . in full dimension, color and movement.[67]

Now I am aware that Spolin's recommendation of the above techniques can be justified in purely practical terms. Visualization of an "inner film" of circumstances is, as Stanislavski also recognized,[68] a great aid to concentration. And relaxation, as every acting teacher I have ever known has emphasized, is a simple physiological precondition of good work.[69] Nonetheless, visualization and relaxation both happen to be standard shamanic preliminaries for a trip to the *illud tempus*. Preparatory ritual sleep is a frequent feature of Ugrian and South American shamanism[70]—not a surprising fact if one bears in mind that dreams are the site of most shamanic experience. And preparatory visualization of the spirits to be visited is practiced by shamans in regions as far remote as Dutch Guiana[71] and Tibet.[72]

Clearly, not everything in shamanism is relevant to acting. Healer of the sick, psychic warrior, tracker-down of strayed souls—all these are important functions of the shaman which are not to our purpose. The only aspect of shamanism that has concerned us is the shaman as contacter and investigator of the *illud tempus*.

It is equally important to recognize that this one relevant aspect of shamanism is only a single—and, at that, a preliminary—aspect of acting. Only in rehearsal or in his warm-up exercises before a performance does the actor function as a shaman. Shamanic techniques are useful only for "getting there" (to the script *illud tempus*). They are of no help in getting the script *illud tempus* down to us. The shaman is expected to "give a long account of all he has seen,"[73] to "tell the audience the results of his journey."[74] But few of us would accept Living Theatre member Steve Ben Israel's definition of the actor as "someone who takes a trip and brings back a message."[75] It is not for messages that we turn to the theatre, but for presence—and here the shaman cannot help us. For an Image to become bodily present, the Image must have a body at its disposal. It is, of course, the actor who provides this body—but not the actor-as-shaman. In order to do the Image this service, the actor must change functions, going from proud venturer to possessed vehicle —from shaman to hungan—in a moment of reversal which I have called the "rounding." But what the rounding is and why it should occur cannot be understood until we have some idea of the state *into* which the actor rounds: that of the divine vehicle, or hungan; that of possession.

Possession seems to be at once unarguably like and unbridgeably different from acting. With respect to the public impression given by possession—that of a body being (rather spookily) lived by a life not its own—it seems a phenomenon clearly related to acting. But, on the other hand, what could be less like the characteristic control and timing of the actor than the automatism of the possessed: helpless, will-less, even (in some cases) lacking consciousness?

In fact, the similarities are still more extensive, and the unlikeness far less significant, than our limited Western idea of possession as a pathological state would ever lead us to believe. The fundamental resemblance does not exhaust the resemblances, and the fundamental "difference" dissolves upon examination.

Since it is the impression he makes on others—that of a body alive with alien life—which most clearly links the possessed with the actor, I shall, as I did with shamanism, put aside the internal experience of the hungan himself for the moment and consider possession in its public function.

Can possession *have* a public function? Is it not, rather, a private affliction? Certainly the examples of possession that have lodged themselves in the Western mind—dybbuk-ridden maidens, hysterical convents, the long line of New Testament demoniacs—seem to be clear instances of mental disease. But in many societies—in Asia, in Africa, in Haiti— possession is not dreaded as a misfortune, but sought after as a religious experience. The force doing the possessing is not regarded as a malign demon intruding itself upon human consciousness, but as a blest god manifesting itself through a human medium.[76] Possession so conceived becomes a precious means of union with the divine.

In such societies the human being capable of possession, the hungan, serves a clear social function, analogous in purpose but opposite in direction to that of the shaman. He makes present among us the world of the gods, the *illud tempus*, which the shaman can only make *himself* present *to*. The trance dancers of Bali, for example, believe that through them celestial beings are able to descend to earth temporarily [77] (*Figure 2*). And among certain North American Indian tribes, "those wearing masks"—the mask being everywhere understood as a symbol of divine possession[78] —"are no longer regarded by the awe-struck crowd as actors and persons representing the gods but as gods themselves descending from heaven to earth."[79]

Figure 2: A possessed Balinese girl performs a pantomimic trance dance (*sangiang*). *Photograph by Gregory Bateson; courtesy of Margaret Mead.*

The analogy between such rituals and theatre performances is not far to seek. In each case, an *illud tempus*—in the ritual, that of the gods; in theatre, that of the Images—is made present through being incarnated by hungans/actors who seem, for the time, to "become" their god/Image. And in fact, anthropologists have frequently employed such terms as "traditional theatre,"[80] "mystery play,"[81] and "operetta"[82] in attempting to convey their impression of a possession ritual. (A Yoruba ceremony I attended certainly came across to me as a dance performance.)[83] One authority goes so far as to assert that possession rituals simply *are* theatre,[84] the possession deities being stock characters, and the hungans, actors trained to portray them.[85]

The objection to this view would seem to be that a possessed person, having delivered himself up to unconscious mental energies, would seem incapable of portraying anything but his own compulsions. However, in societies where possession is a religion, merely personal manifestations on the part of the possessed are not considered acceptable: "Unlike a hysteric who shows his own misery and desires by means of a symptom—which is an entirely personal form of expression— the man who is ritually possessed must correspond to the traditional conception of some mythical personage."[86] These "traditional conceptions" are taught to new cult-members,[87] each of whom generally learns several gods so as to be able to serve as a teacher himself at some later date.[88] Particular gods are assigned to particular cult-members, either on a permanent basis or on the occasion of each possession ceremony.[89] Indeed, the very order in which the gods may incarnate themselves is likely to be fixed by tradition.[90]

Where such practices prevail, it is natural that the pantheon of possession deities should come to be looked upon as a kind of repertoire of dramatic roles, comparable, as Leiris observes,[91] to the traditional masks of the *commedia dell'arte*. Each possession deity has a distinct personality type and mode of behavior:

> *Ogun*, god of blacksmiths, warriors, hunters, and all who use iron, is characterized by coarse and energetic manners; *Shango*, god of thunder, by manly and jolly dances; *Orishala*,

the creator god, by calm and serene behaviour; *Shapana*, god of smallpox and the contagious diseases, by restless agitation; *Eshu Elegba*, messenger of the other gods, by cynical and abusive attitudes.[92]

What is more, each is imagined as being eternally in the process of repeating some single action or course of action[93] which, immediately upon being possessed by him, the hungan launches into performing: "*Zatao* covers his head with dust and eats earth; *Nyalya*, on the other hand, being a coquette, shakes off the dust which soils her; *Sadyara*, who is a serpent, creeps on the ground; *Dongo*, the spirit of thunder, points to the sky and growls."[94] These snippets of action are often episodes from a myth associated with the possessing deity: "If Aira [takes possession of a hungan] during the time when [another hungan] is already possessed by Oxalá, then 'Aira' immediately sets about helping 'Oxalá' to walk, carrying 'Oxalá' in his arms as if the latter had had his limbs broken: thus he acts out the Myth of the Water of Oxalá."[95] We can see in such action-fragments a parallel to the ever-occurring events of a script *illud tempus*, which an actor brings among us by bringing those who are forever enacting them into our midst.

And just as in the theatre something other than an individual human figure can function as an Image, so in a possession cult virtually anything that the members happen to be preoccupied with—an animal,[96] an ethnic trait (e. g., "Polishness"),[97] an abstract pattern of movement (e. g., European dancing),[98] even a machine (pump, bush clearer, motorboat)[99]—may come to be regarded as a possession god.

As was the case with linking acting and shamanism,[100] the attempt to establish the actor as a kind of hungan gains in plausibility from the circumstance that, in many cultures, the hungan is a kind of actor. And again as in the case of shamanism, it is difficult to think of a single scenic aspect of theatre that is not also an aspect of hunganic ritual.

Mimed action and spoken dialogue are fully as characteristic of the hungan's as of the shaman's performance. The human vehicle of the Ethiopian *zar* (possession god), Azzaj Deho is expected to be able to reproduce, in his dances, the coughing, wheezing, and froglike hopping which are thought to be characteristic of that strange deity.[101] In fact, a whole vocabulary of stylized gestures is associated with each of the *zars*, as with each character in the Noh or Kathakali theatres.[102] Similarly, one possessed by a voodoo *loa* is expected to reflect the god's temperament in his gestures, even to the extent of performing acrobatic dances if appropriate.[103] The hungan-as-*loa* holds long dialogues with other priests and bystanders, which often take on the quality of dramatic interludes.[104] This sort of thing demands that the Haitian hungan be fairly skilled at vocal imitation. Indeed, total and eerie transformation of the voice seems to be a universal characteristic of possession experience.[105]

Like shamanic rituals, hunganic rites make extensive use of such scenic elements as costumes, properties, music, and even make-up. In Haiti and Ethiopia possession is the occasion for adornment and disguise.[106] Each *zar* and *loa* has his traditional costume, and each his traditional prop (sword, stick, bottle, cigar), which is brought out to his hungan at the first sign of possession.[107] Music, especially drum music, is the indispensable background for all voodoo rites, its function being that of a stimulant.[108] And in at least one possession cult, among the Vezo of Madagascar, the worshipper paints onto his face a pattern of circles and bars associated with the particular *tsūmba* (possession spirit) that he wishes to incarnate.[109] There would seem to be an analogy here with the assignment of a traditional facial make-up to each character-type in the Kathakali and classical Chinese theatres.

As I indicated earlier, shamanic ritual displays two sure signs of dramatic impulse: interpolated comic scenes and additional actors. Both tendencies are, if anything, even more pronounced in hunganic rite, as is clear from the following accounts:

> Whenever a depressing atmosphere develops as a result of the violence of possessions, then Guédé [one of the *loa*] appears, puckish and obscene. He sits on girls' knees and pretends to be about to rape them. The congregation revels in this sort of fun and laughs heartily.[110]

> What else can it be called except "theatre" when the possessed turn the simultaneous manifestation of several gods in different people into an organized "impromptu"? These impromptus, which vary in style, are much appreciated by the audience. . . . Take an example: someone possessed by Zaka appears under the peristyle in the get-up of a peasant. By canny movements he mimes the anxiety of a countryman come to town, and who fears to be robbed. Now another possessed person joins him, one might almost say "comes on." It is Guédé-*nibo*, of the Guédé family, which watches over the dead. Zaka is clearly terrified by the presence of his gloomy colleague and tries to propitiate him, inviting him to have something to eat and to drink some rum.[111]

No less than his shamanic counterpart, the hungan is likely to have the talents and temperament of an actor— in fact, may first have been invited to join the cult on that very basis. An expressive body, a taste for spectacle, and a gift for imitation are the qualities for which a *Bori*-woman is selected, and are the qualities she must cultivate if she wishes to achieve "star" ranking in the cult.[112] Along with these gifts are likely to go the usual "star" personality traits of pride, aggressiveness, and insistence on one's prerogatives.[113] Nor am I forcing the comparison for the sake of an analogy with theatre: the use of the word "star" (French: *vedette*) to designate the leading figures in a possession cult originates with anthropological observers of the cults themselves.[114]

If the participants in a possession cult behave much like actors, the person in charge of the cult in many ways resembles a producer-director. The *Bori jakeso* coaches initiates down to the slightest nuances of their god-roles.[115] The Songhay *zima* assigns parts, conducts the orchestra, prompts cult-members on the attributes of the god they are about to be possessed by, cues in spectacular effects at the right moment—and takes charge of dividing up the take (of offerings) afterwards.[116] These impresarios do the advance organizing for, and then themselves often "host," the ceremonies they have arranged.[117] They themselves may or may not be susceptible to possession[118]—just as a Western director may or may not also work as an actor.

Finally, the viewpoint of the congregation at possession ceremonies is in large part that of a theatre audience. Spectators distinguish between good and mediocre dancers, comment on exceptionally fine singing or drum-work, and so forth.[119]

But as in linking shamanism and acting, it is not enough to show that in some peripheral respects hunganism is theatrical. We want to know whether in any essential respect acting is hunganic.

Some anthropologists have gone so far as to suggest that we must look to possession rites for the historical origins of theatre:

> Surely it is at least possible that the real impulse to the drama lay not wholly in 'goat-songs' and 'circular dancing places' but also in the cardinal, the essentially dramatic, conviction of the religion of Dionysus, that the worshipper can not only worship, but can become, can *be* his god. Athene and Zeus and Poseidon have no drama because no one, in his wildest moments, believed he could become and be Athene or Zeus or Poseidon. It is indeed only in the orgiastic religions that these splendid moments of conviction could come, and, for Greece at least, only in an orgiastic religion did the drama take its rise.[120]

Such a view receives confirmation from the extraordinary relationship that exists between the Malay shadow play and Malay spirit mediumship:

> Some of the puppet characters in the shadow play, such as Arjuna, may appear as powerful spirits in a spirit medium performance. Conversely, a shadow play is a ritual per-

formance, with incense and offerings to the spirits symbol-
ised by the puppet characters. Sometimes there is also a
mediumistic performance in the dawn at the end of the
shadow play, with the puppet master possessed by the spirits
of some of his puppets. Night after night he has manipu-
lated them; in compensation as it were before they are shut
away again they manipulate him.[121]

In another instance of such reciprocity, the classic Vietnamese
theatre is known to have borrowed certain conventions of
movement from the expressive vocabulary of local possession
cults.[122]

All this is very striking, but there seems to be one insuper-
able difficulty. When we turned our attention from the public
role of the shaman to the shaman's inner experience of that
role, we found the inner experience to be as closely related to
acting as the public role had proved. But when we turn in
like manner to the inner experience of the hungan, we at once
strike up against what would appear to be a block to any
further comparisons with the actor. Obliteration of consciousness and will by the possessing force seems to be the
very essence of a possession experience, whereas acting is
dependent for its very existence on self-awareness, memory,
and will.

Actually, this is an oversimplification all around. The
possessed hungan may lose consciousness, but he may also
enter a strange state of double consciousness in which he is,
and is not, himself. *Any of these psychic states are also
possibilities for the actor in performance.* In fact, a shared
spectrum of possible states of consciousness is one of the most
significant similarities between the hungan and the actor.

It is a prime tenet—or, if you prefer, convention—of most
possession cults that consciousness is totally extinguished
during possession. Upon returning to himself, the hungan
invariably claims to remember nothing of what he felt or
did while the god rode him.[123] The same claim is often advanced in pathological possessions.[124]

Obliterated consciousness would seem to be not only an impossible but an undesirable state for an actor: What would become of his indispensable control and recall? Yet most performers have had moments on the stage when they could say with Living Theatre member Steve Ben Israel, "I didn't know where I was."[125] As I pointed out earlier,[126] while not all approaches to acting are equally shamanic, all are to some extent in touch with the practice of shamanism. The same could be said of the relation between different acting techniques and the experience of possession. Even such presentational actors as Charles Dullin, Louis Jouvet, and Jean-Louis Barrault have testified to the experience of being taken over by a character they were playing.[127] At the moment of entering her creative state, Sarah Bernhardt would cry: "Dieu est venu!"[128]—the very words with which a hungan might greet the onset of possession. And while the popular idea of the Stanislavski actor "losing himself" in the part is quite mistaken, he too knows moments when "your head will swim from the excitement of the sudden and complete fusion of your life with your part. It may not last long but while it does you will be incapable of distinguishing between yourself and the person you are portraying."[129] Still, however much like possession this experience may sound, the climax of creative energy which it is here said to bring the actor would seem to be a very different thing from the hungan's climax of self-loss. But a striking circumstance links them. In the very instant of hunganic self-obliteration there often appear in the possessed person unsuspected energies and gifts *for performance*. For example: "The dances which he executed, now and also later, were very finished ones in which he showed much grace and elegance, accompanied by bows, etc. It should be noted that the possessed man had never in his life before put one foot before the other to dance."[130] Such a phenomenon justifies us in suspecting that there may be profound resemblances between the psychic structures of hunganism and acting.

Consciousness is not invariably or completely obliterated in possession. Just as some actors have more "internal" work methods than others, so different hungans are capable of different degrees of trance.[131] And just as an actor may be more "in it" at one performance than another, so a hungan may enter more or less deeply into trance on different occasions,[132] or even at different moments of the same ceremony.[133]

In other words, the possessed person may be characterized by that very state of dual consciousness which characterizes the actor in performance: the feeling that one is "somebody else," combined with the awareness that it is oneself who is feeling that way:

> Hélène [a medium] has more than once told me that she has had the impression of becoming and of momentarily being Leopold. . . . she first has a fugitive vision of her cavalier, and then he seems to pass gradually into her, she feels him as it were invade and penetrate her whole organic substance as if he became herself or she him. It is, in short, a spontaneous incarnation *without loss of consciousness or memory*.[134] [italics mine]

> I was obliged almost without ceasing to utter cries, weep, sing, dance, and roll upon the ground where I went into horrible contortions; I was forced to jerk my head and feet in all directions, howl like a bear. . . . *I am never absent, I always know what I am doing or saying*.[135] [italics mine]

Some possession religions have elaborate "two-soul theories" which might explain such phenomena. Man is believed to have both an individual soul (*karfe, êini, biya*, or *gros bon ange*) and also a less personal vital principle (*kurwa, ori, hunde*, or *ti-bon ange*). In possession, it is the personal soul which is displaced by the possessing god; the vital principle remains in the body all the while.[136] Thus a loophole is left for consciousness. The loophole that Stanislavski leaves for consciousness in the actor also relies upon a kind of "two-soul theory": "An actor is split into two parts when he is acting. You recall how Tommaso Salvini put it: 'An actor lives, weeps, laughs on the stage, but as he weeps and laughs he observes his own tears and mirth. It is this double existence, this balance between life and acting, that makes for art.'"[137]

It may still be easier to see why double consciousness must characterize the actor—at least the actor in any sort of emotional touch with his role—than how it can be present in the wholly taken-over hungan. The difficulty vanishes, however—and the similarity between actor and hungan stands forth—if we bear in mind that what both the actor and the hungan are possessed *by*, while it may feel other to them, is in fact some aspect of their own psyches. There is nothing surprising in the fact that a possession-force should be felt as copresent with the self; it *is* (an element of) the self.

If there is nowhere but within for the shaman (and the actor-as-shaman) to pursue his journey, there are nothing but inner impulses for the hungan (and the actor-as-hungan) to be possessed by.

From a medical point of view, there can be no doubt that possession is a crisis within the life of the mind, though authorities disagree as to the nature and extent of the crisis. Freud, seeing possession as the return of rejected and repressed impulses, identified it as a form of neurosis.[138] Later observers, noting that the behavior of possessed people displays "gross non-reality ideation, abnormal perceptual experiences [and] profound emotional upheavals," have gone so far as to characterize possession as schizoid,[139] whereas Métraux has pointed out that "the symptoms of the opening phase of trance . . . conform exactly, in their main features, to the stock clinical conception of hysteria":

> People possessed start by giving an impression of having lost control of their motor system. Shaken by spasmodic convulsions, they pitch forward, as though projected by a spring, turn frantically around and around, stiffen and stay still with body bent forward, sway, stagger, save themselves, again lose balance, only to fall finally in a state of semiconsciousness.[140]

The psychotherapist Rollo May suggests clinical redefinitions for the old terms "daimon" and "daimonic possession." "Daimon" he defines as "any natural function in the individual that has the power of taking over the whole person"; "daimonic possession" can then be understood as the takeover of the entire personality by one of these powerful functions.[141] What leads the "daimon," so defined, to realize its ever-present potential for take-over is its having been denied its rightful role in mental life—that is, its having been repressed.[142] An impulse so denied eventually returns with redoubled force and totally swamps the personality that had refused it even the limited role in mental life to which it was entitled.

This explanation, even while rejecting the literal existence of any exterior possessing forces (*zars*, *loa*, or whatever), makes clear why the inner forces actually responsible for possession should be experienced as external. The possessed person projects the inner drive that possesses him as "other" —sometimes as another person,[143] more often as a god or spirit—precisely *because* he cannot acknowledge it as an aspect of himself. Its otherness is a metaphor for his mind's disavowal of it.

But why should the repressed drive be projected in the exalted form of a god or spirit? In assigning the rejected element such high status, the possessed person is paying unconscious tribute to the role it could play in healing the mind that has rejected it.[144] For only by reaccepting the banished impulse and restoring it to the position it should never have lost, can the possessed person hope to regain mental balance.[145] This recognition is present in the possession religions themselves. In the Nigerian *Bori* cult, for example, sickness is thought to be caused by a normally good "white" god that has turned "black" (i. e., been disavowed); but once the sick woman accepts possession *by this very deity*, then he, the "black" god, is believed to turn "white" again and she is cured.[146] When a possessed mind projects the element of itself that it has repressed as a salvationary deity with whom it wishes union, it is unconsciously acknowledging that (re)union with that rejected element could be its salvation.

This last point answers the challenge which May's view of possession as intrapsychic might seem to receive from the fact, noted earlier, that "far from expressing *himself*, the possessed tries to personify some mythological being whose character on the whole is foreign to him."[147] It rather confirms than sheds doubt on the inner origin of possession-forces that they seek to attach themselves to traditional god-figures. Only a traditional god is regarded by the possessed as sufficiently powerful to stand in his mind as a symbol of the healing power he unconsciously assigns to the rejected impulse.

We have now seen enough of the psychic mechanisms of possession to understand in what way they parallel the inner experience of the actor. The actor, too, must put his body at the disposal of psychic components normally repressed and inaccessible to him. In Grotowski's theatre, for example, the actor's very aim is

> to eliminate his organism's resistance to this psychic process. The result is freedom from the time-lapse between inner impulse and outer reaction in such a way that the impulse is already an outer reaction. Impulse and action are concurrent: the body vanishes, burns, and the spectator sees only a series of visible impulses.[148]

It may well be that it was from his "personal ideal," Stanislavski,[149] that Grotowski learned to value above all else in an actor this hunganic availability to unconscious impulse; for the great Russian director, too, undertook to teach actors "how, without thinking, to surrender yourself instantly and utterly into the power of intuition and inspiration."[150] And indeed, all of Stanislavski's specific techniques—emotion memory, physical actions, objectives, "ifs"—are nothing more than lures to encourage the actor's unconscious feelings to rise and "possess" his body with that special, decisive energy that only long repressed impulses can impart:

Do as a hunter does in stalking game. If a bird does not rise of its own accord you would never find it among all the leaves of the forest. You have to coax it out, whistle to it, use various *lures*.

Our artistic emotions are, at first, as shy as wild animals and they hide in the depths of our souls. . . . All you can do is to concentrate your attention on the most effective kind of lure for them.[151]

It should now be clear why actors often do their best work in roles far removed from their own personalities: the green-room clown excels in tough-guy parts; the shy girl is startlingly effective as the vamp. In such instances the role becomes a much needed opportunity for usually repressed aspects of personality to claim their place in a mind accustomed to disowning them. The same tendency is evident in possession rituals. "Not uncommonly . . . devotees are possessed by *loa* whose character is the very opposite of their own. Trance, then, acts as a form of compensation."[152]

Of course, if nothing in an actor's overt *or* repressed nature affords him a point of contact with an Image, then that is one Image he can never be possessed by, whatever the apparent similarities of age, *emploi* and so forth. "The roles for which you haven't the appropriate feelings are those you will never play well," Stanislavski warned his first-year class. Both this recognition and the conclusion that Stanislavski goes on to draw from it—"Actors are not in the main divided by types . . . [but] by their inner qualities"[153]—are reflected in the practice of possession religions. Hungans generally choose one god or class of god to specialize in;[154] and the basis for that choice is much more likely to be a worshipper's feeling of temperamental affinity for the god than any physical or visual similarity between them.[155]

Hungan and actor both submit to being taken over by rejected, and hence unconscious, aspects of their personalities. But as in the case of shamanism, the resemblance extends beyond a general similarity to specific similarities of technique.

In particular, three of Stanislavski's "lures" for the unconscious seem to have clear analogues (sources?) in hunganic techniques for encouraging the rise of those psychic forces by which the hungan seeks to be possessed. These are: relaxation of muscles, use of physical objects, and use of physical actions.

Relaxation of muscles, which I have already considered as an analogue to the shaman's ritual sleep, also plays a role in the possession phase of acting. Stanislavski warns that "muscular tautness *interferes* with inner emotional experience"; tense muscles "*impede* your actions" [italics mine].[156] As the body's sign (and means) of *resistance* to possessing impulses, muscular tension is the first of those "blocks" at the eradication of which, according to Grotowski, training of the actor-as-hungan must aim.[157] Relaxation of muscles is also an essential preliminary of actual possession experience. "Trance is preceded by a sleepy condition. The possessed cannot keep his eyes open and seems overcome with a vague languor."[158]

Although sometimes skeptical about the wisdom of working from the outside in,[159] Stanislavski recognized the value of physical objects and physical actions in facilitating take-over by the unconscious. One day the student actor Kostya comes across a mysterious old morning coat and slips it on. The effect is to release in him a stream of unconscious impulses so strong as to precipitate a true possession experience:

> From that moment on and right up tc the time of the masquerade, which was set for three days later, something was going on inside of me: I was not I, in the sense of my usual consciousness of myself. Or, to be more precise, I was not alone but with someone I sought in myself and could not find. . . .
> Finally in the night I suddenly woke up and everything was clear. That second life which I had been leading parallel to my usual one was a secret, subconscious life. In it there was going on the work of searching for that mildewed man whose clothes I had accidentally found.[160]

It should come as no surprise that physical objects often serve precisely the same function in possession ceremonies. Leiris tells of an Ethiopian hungan who, as a result of playing with a policeman's gun, was successively possessed by two warrior *zars*.[161] The following practice has a particularly close parallel with the Stanislavski incident, since here, too, the object used to induce possession is an article of clothing:

> A loin-cloth is placed on the [hungan's] head, covering it entirely. . . . After several moments the loin-cloth is removed: the metamorphosis has been effected. The god is there, with all his characteristics: a certain gait, a special voice, codified gestures.[162]

"From believing in the truth of one small [physical] action," Stanislavski told his students, "an actor can come to feel himself in his part and to have faith in the reality of a whole play."[163] Why this should be so he explains at another point in his writings: "As you are *drawn* to physical actions you are *drawn away* from the life of your subconscious. In that way you render it free to act and *induce* it to work creatively."[164] In other words, having a physical action to accomplish puts the body off its guard and allows the possessing impulses to take over. The avowedly anti-Stanislavski Open Theatre company do not part company with Stanislavski on this point; they, too, recognize that "action . . . engages emotion rather than the other way round."[165] Such techniques find a hunganic precedent in Ethiopian possession religion, where "one of the most frequently used means for putting oneself into a trance is . . . the deliberate imitation of movements associated with the opening phases of possession."[166]

Another parallel between acting and possession can be inferred from the similarity between an acting exercise of Grotowski's and a possession phenomenon observed by Ambroise Paré:

> Choose an emotional impulse (such as crying) and transfer it to a particular part of the body—a foot, for example—

which then has to give it expression. . . . Express two contrasting impulses with two different parts of the body: the hands laugh while the feet cry.[167]

A young gentleman used from time to time to fall into a certain convulsion, having now the left arm alone, now a single finger, now one thigh, now both, now the backbone and the whole body so suddenly shaken and tormented by this convulsion that only with great difficulty could four menservants hold him down in bed.[168]

Of course, Grotowski is concerned with a conscious practice, Paré with an hysterical symptom. But to train the body to reflect psychic impulse as specifically and spontaneously (though not, of course, as compulsively) as in hysteria is precisely Grotowski's goal.[169]

Here is a final and vivid illustration of how alike the psychic experiences of acting and possession can be. Dressed in that morning coat which, as we have already seen, stirred up such unsuspected depths in him, Stanislavski's student Kostya goes forth to encounter his teachers, the directors Tortsov and Rakhmanov:

"Can it be you—Kostya? What are you supposed to be?"

"A critic!" I answered in a hoarse voice, and with sharp diction.

"What critic, my boy?" Rakhmanov continued his query, somewhat taken aback by my bold and penetrating glance.

I felt like a leech clinging to him.

"What critic?" I retorted with obvious intent to insult him. "The fault-finding critic who lives inside of Kostya Nazvanov. I live in him in order to interfere with his work. That is my great joy. That is the purpose of my existence."

I was myself amazed at the brazen, unpleasant tone and the fixed, cynical, rude stare which accompanied it, and with which I addressed Rakhmanov.

. . .

"Let's go," he finally said rather uncertainly. "The others have long since begun."

"Let's go, then, since they have long since begun," I mimicked his words and did not budge but continued to stare brazenly at my disconcerted instructor.

. . .

Here to my complete surprise I let out a shrill squeak instead of a guffaw. I was quite taken aback myself, it was so unexpected. Evidently too it had quite an effect on Tortsov.

"What the —— " he began to exclaim, then added, "You come over here, closer to the footlights."

I moved over in a sinister, ambling gait.

"What critic are you?" asked Tortsov, probing me with his eyes as if he did not recognize me. "Critic of what?"

"Of the person I live with," I rasped.

"Who is that?" pursued Tortsov.

"Kostya," I said.

"Have you gotten under his skin?" Tortsov knew just the right cues to give me.

"Indeed, yes!"

"Who let you do it?"

"He did."[170]

We have no difficulty in recognizing the "critic . . . of the person I live with" as an ordinarily repressed, now suddenly dominant, component of Kostya's personality. We note also the presence of that doubled consciousness which we have found to be characteristic of possession experience: "While I was playing the part of the Critic I still did not lose the sense of being myself . . . . I divided myself, as it were, into two personalities. One continued as an actor, the other was an observer.[171] We hear in the "Critic's" sharp replies to Torstov an echo of such conversations between demon and exorcist as:

Brendel. Do you also know the traitor Judas?

The Devil [in a twelve-year-old serving girl]. He sits beside me in hell.

B. Did you also know the unrepentant Thief, Pilate, Herod, Dr. Johannes Faustus . . . ?

D. Oh, they are my best friends. I have in hell the letter of Faust written with his blood.

B. Does it not burn?

D. Oh no!

B. Of what use is it to you?

D. I must have it so that I may produce it and convict him thereby.[172]

And finally, we observe how, in true hungan fashion, Kostya experiences some difficulty in shaking off his *loa:*

> As I walked home I caught myself repeating the gestures and gait of the character whose image I had created. But that was not all. During dinner with my landlady and the other boarders I was captious, scoffing and irritable —unlike myself but very like my carping Critic. Even my landlady noticed this.[173]

Once allowed up into consciousness, a repressed impulse is reluctant to seek the darkness once more.

"Strangely enough," the young actor concludes, looking back over his experience, "this duality did not impede, it actually promoted my creative work."[174] Perhaps by now we have seen enough of the affinity between possession and acting not to share Kostya's impression of strangeness.

An incidental advantage of the shaman and hungan analogies I have been developing is that they suggest a vocabulary for evaluating the work of actors. "Too shamanic" might describe acting that shows evidence of an intelligent approach to the Image, but lacks abandonment to the psychic impulses encountered in that investigation. "Too hunganic" might be the verdict on acting that puts itself fully at the Image's disposal, but does not precede that surrender with sufficiently careful investigation to guarantee that the impulses surrendered to are the appropriate ones.

I am, however, hardly in a position to set about faulting actors for not making the right transition between the shamanic and hunganic phases of their work, when I have myself as yet said nothing about this transition, beyond describing it as a "rounding," and declaring it to be the moment in which the theatre, as an event, is born.

We can best approach the connection between the shamanic and hunganic aspects of acting by considering the connection between shamanism and possession themselves.

But is there any connection? A number of authorities, most notably Mircea Eliade, insist on the distinctness of shamanism from possession experience:

> It will easily be seen wherein a shaman differs from a "possessed" person, for example; the shaman controls his "spirits," in the sense that he, a human being, is able to communicate with the dead, "demons," and "nature spirits," without thereby becoming their instrument.[175]

It would seem, no matter what empirical evidence might be brought forward, that the psychological structures of the two experiences exclude each other: ascent of a man to the gods, on the one hand; descent of a god into a man, on the other.

Nonetheless, there is overwhelming evidence (much of it to be found in Eliade's own book) that "this distinction is in fact untenable," and that "shamanism and spirit possession regularly occur together."[176] The Songhay, for example, believe that it is the same "second soul" (*biya*) that wanders abroad on shamanic dream-quests which is displaced in possession experiences—a theory that certainly seems to imply the susceptibility of shamans to possession.[177] Even in societies where "shaman" and "hungan" are separate functions, normally fulfilled by different persons, it is not unheard of for practitioners of these specialties to exchange roles now and again. Thus in Laos the shaman (*mo thévada*) occasionally takes part in possession rituals, while conversely, the possession priestess (*nang thiem*) sometimes sends forth her soul on shamanic missions.[178]

As concepts, mutually exclusive; as phenomena, hardly ever to be found apart: What are we to make of this paradox?

An important clue is provided by the fact that shamanism and possession employ a common symbol for the encounter with the *illud tempus*: that of horseback riding.

> The "horse" is employed by the shaman, in various contexts, as a means of achieving ecstasy, that is, the "coming out of oneself" that makes the mystical journey possible. . . . The

"horse" enables the shaman to fly through the air, to reach the heavens. . . . The horse is a mythical image of death and hence is incorporated into the ideologies and techniques of ecstasy. The horse carries the deceased into the beyond; it produces a "break-through in plane," the passage from this world to other worlds.[179]

A *loa* is spoken of as "mounting" or "saddling" his *chual* (horse). Possession being closely linked with dancing, it is also thought of in terms of a spirit "dancing in the head of his horse." It is also an invasion of the body by a supernatural spirit; hence the often used expression: "the *loa* is seizing his horse."[180]

Of course, the horse-and-rider symbolism is applied in precisely opposite senses in the two passages: the shaman is the rider *to* the gods, the hungan is the "ridden" *of* the gods. But there would seem to be some significance in the fact that it is a *single* symbol that gets reversed. If shamanism and hunganism can both be contained within the implications of a single symbol, does not that argue some underlying continuity between them? The implication is clear: shamanism and possession are not two wholly separate ways of encountering the divine, but are the two moments or stages of a single encounter. The shaman, masterful rider to the gods, at some point goes over to being the hungan, masterfully ridden by the gods. We are still a long way from being able to explain why this rounding—this change of role, which is also a change of direction—should take place; but we are at least in a position to view it as a moment within a single continuous event.

As further evidence of this continuity, it should be recalled that the mythic space through which the shaman ascends and that through which the possession god descends are one and the same space. Or, to put it another way, the road from heaven to earth is a two-way street[181] and is regarded as such even within shamanism itself. "It is by dragging the gods down to his own level, as much as by soaring aloft to meet them, that the shaman enables man to deal with his deities on an equal footing."[182] So among the Manasi, while shamans possess the usual "ecstatic capacities . . . to make mystical journeys to the sky to meet the gods directly and convey men's prayers to them," nevertheless, "sometimes it is the god who descends into the ceremonial hut."[183] An extreme instance of flexibility on this point is the attitude of the Eskimos toward their goddess Sedna: "The idea of the journey to Sedna and of summoning Sedna, or being possessed by Sedna, seem to be interchangeable."[184]

What leads the gods to rush down upon the shaman who is seeking them? It almost seems as if they are *provoked* into doing so by the shamanic quest itself, as if *in response*. By going up to the god, the shaman brings the god down on himself—and so brings about his own possession. Among the ancient Chinese, magical flight was considered "the cause of [possession] by the *shen* and not its *result*; it was because a man was already able to 'rise to higher spheres' . . . that 'intelligent *shen* descended into' him."[185] Among the Ngadju Dyak of Southern Borneo, shamans become possessed by the gods only after they have made a mystical sky-journey to the gods' "village."[186] And among the Serapic mystics of ancient Egypt, the deity by whom the worshipper longed to be possessed he first sought out in his dreams[187]—a clear case of shamanic quest serving as a preliminary to divine possession.

Why the rounding of shaman as hungan occurs can be understood from the moment *when* it occurs: not at any point along the shamanic arc, but at the peak point—the moment when the quest can go no further, the spirits be held no longer, the magic accomplish no more. To "round" at that moment—to become a hungan, a mere vehicle—is the price the shaman must pay for having attained his goal. "Through his constant struggling with . . . spirits, he falls at last into their power, that is, he ends by being really possessed."[188] This is surrender, if you will, but a surrender that consummates all that has gone before. The shaman's yielding up of his body to the possessing force is but the final step in achieving that union with it which he has sought from the start.

This concept of the rounding as a surrender consummating a quest is clearly applicable to the experience of the actor.

That shamanic quest and hunganic surrender are but two stages of a single encounter is, if anything, even clearer when it is not literal shamans and hungans we are talking about, but the actor-as-shaman and the actor-as-hungan. There is no longer any problem of different orders of "gods" demanding different modes of encounter: some to be ascended to, some to be received in descent. That component of his personality which the actor-as-shaman has all along been moving toward is the very thing by which, as hungan, he is ultimately to be possessed. To speak of a shamanic "quest" which is a separable preliminary to the actor's experience of possession is perhaps not quite accurate. What the actor "seeks" is, precisely, the experience of possession itself. That is, he seeks to encourage those of his inner impulses which are relevant to the role to emerge as dominant; and to encourage the domination of the whole personality by one part is to invite possession, as (following Rollo May) I have defined it.

The rounding is simply the moment when this take-over, so long striven for, finally occurs. The Stanislavski actor who, in rehearsal and preperformance exercises, goes in search of particular unconscious impulses in order that he may be, at a certain moment, possessed by them, illustrates the total pattern of the actor-shaman rounding as the actor-hungan. But a still more striking example of a rounding is contained in the following statement (quoted in part earlier) by one of the actors of the Living Theatre:

> We call it a "trans-flip" because we don't have a better word for it. Everybody sits in a circle and breathes towards the performer, sends him positive energy. And the objective of this trans-flip is for the organism to go into the visionary stage. The whole concept is that the person is the visionary and it's from him that we can take a trip. And if we sit around him and take positive vibrations and breathe on him, we can have that experience with him. I had six minutes and I felt I needed thirty seconds in the existential world. I needed thirty seconds there to create a certain type of energy ex-

plosion within my own being. In other words, I was reliving
certain traumas, certain experiences. And as one does that,
it keys off in his whole system a fantastic energy explosion.
This is done in a ritualistic way, internally and externally.

So in my own experience, I waited for that point and all
of a sudden, it was like, Oh my God. When that happened,
I just flew. And I stuck, moving with the dynamic of the explosion. What happened after a few minutes was that the
room spinned this way and then spinned that way at the same
time. I didn't know where I was. I was going, going, going,
moving in this dynamic, signalling, communicating, not ter-
ribly aware of what I was doing, just being out there, being
out there waiting for something else to happen when the
signal came that this is as far as you can go out there at this
moment. And what happens is another explosion and it lands
you—you don't land it, it lands you. You surrender to it. It
really lands you.[189]

Here we have the whole process I have been examining in
this chapter—shamanic quest →rounding →hunganic possession—not only clearly present in a single experience, but described in terms that clearly link it with actual shamanic and
hunganic practice.

A community ("everybody") desires the presence of the
illud tempus ("the existential world"). They choose the actor
as their vicarious journeyer to it ("it's from him that we can
take a trip"), and entrust him with their longing inquiry
("Everybody sits in a circle and breathes toward the performer, sends him positive energy"). The actor sets out on
his shamanic voyage ("organism go[es] into the visionary
stage") to the *illud tempus*, which, as simultaneously without
and within, is simultaneously approached "internally and externally" by means of shamanic magic flight ("just flew . . .
going, going, going, moving in the dynamic . . . just being
out there").

Then, when the high point of the shamanic arc is reached
("as far as you can go out there at this moment"), "something
else . . . happen[s]": namely, the rounding. Suddenly the actor-
shaman is caught up in the world of energy he has sought

("another explosion") and is overmastered by it ("it lands you —you don't land it, it lands you"). He has completed his mission by rounding as the possessed vehicle, the actor-hungan ("You surrender to it. It really lands you"), in, and by, whom the *illud tempus* is presented.

We have thus far avoided the question of what it is like for the others present when an actor rounds—that is, what it means to be "rounded *upon*." This amounts to asking what it means to be an audience. For if the rounding is the defining act of performance, and in it, theatre is born, then in our response to it we are born as a theatre audience.

CHAPTER 3

The Audience

I shall begin my consideration of theatre audiences by returning to an incident I discussed in the previous chapter for the light it shed on the experience of the actor; but this time my emphasis will be on the kind of experience it provided for those who were its audience. Kostya's two teachers, Tortsov and Rakhmanov, react very differently to the "possession" of their student by the Image of the Carping Critic.[1] Tortsov seems delighted, and even feeds the "Critic" cues. But Rakhmanov is strangely thrown: Kostya has the impression that he is "somewhat taken aback by my bold and penetrating glance" and would like "to get this incident over with as quickly as possible but [does] not know how to go about it."[2]

Now this is very strange. For Rakhmanov is a stern, demanding pedagogue, and Kostya, as a rule, goes in fear of him. But the situation is reversed—now it is the young actor who causes his teacher uneasiness—when his teacher becomes his audience.

At first we may be inclined to attribute this to the prickliness of the character Kostya was playing, the "brazen, unpleasant tone," "fixed cynical . . . stare," and "sinister, ambling gait."[3] But if we think about it for a moment, we realize that we have all had similar sensations of uneasiness in the presence of actors, irrespective of the role they happened to be playing. A friend—even a child—puts on a mask, even a comic mask, and we no longer feel quite comfortable with him. An actress we know has just come offstage; she has given a splendid performance, but we are not at all anxious to be with her just then. The spectator in the next seat turns out to be an audience "plant"; comes the intermission, we give him a wide berth. It would seem that there is something in the actor-audience relationship itself, quite apart from the content of particular performances, that creates uneasiness in the spectator.

How has uneasiness crept into our relations with one who is, after all, our own appointee (for it is we who have dispatched the actor-shaman on his quest)? The audiences of actual shamans are not uneasy but eager.[4] They encourage their shaman in his encounter with the divine,[5] and, on his return from the *illud tempus*, greet him with cries of "let us hear!"[6]

However, we must remember that something happens to the actor-shaman between the time we dispatch him and the time we are disconcerted by him. He "rounds," becomes the possessed hungan; and it is *that* being—that body lived by a life not its own—that we are made uncomfortable by. Our uneasiness with the actor, like Rakhmanov's with Kostya, dates from the moment of his passing from shaman to possessed. And even then, uneasiness does not constitute the whole of our response: we do not, after all, run panic-stricken from the theatre. We feel a good deal of Tortsov's eager curiosity, along with Rakhmanov's discomfort. The response of an audience to an actor is a profoundly ambivalent one; and the sources of that ambivalence, which I shall now trace, lie partly in the nature of Images, partly in the kind of figure the actor is, partly in the kind of group an audience is, and partly in the nature of the theatrical event.

If we compare the uneasiness that theatre audiences feel toward possessed actors with the attitude of the congregation at a possession rite toward its hungans, the first thing that strikes us is a contrast. Worshippers in Haitian and African possession cults seem not only unintimidated by, but even quite familiar and easy with, possessed persons. They exert themselves to provide a physically and emotionally secure atmosphere for the hungan,[7] have no qualms about reaching out a hand to calm him if necessary,[8] and are even, as we have seen, capable of being amused by him.[9] Indeed, all class-B voodoo movies notwithstanding, the prevailing atmosphere at most possession ceremonies is good-humored[10] and casual;[11] the *ambiance* is almost that of a cabaret.[12]

On closer examination, however, an even more acute form of that ambivalence which characterizes theatre audiences' response to their actor-hungans is seen to afflict possession-congregations: if their casualness toward the possessed is more apparent, their uneasiness before him is also more profound.[13] In part, this uneasiness is due to the fact that a possessed person is often physically dangerous. Possession is the take-over of the whole personality by repressed impulses, and the impulses most likely to be repressed are hostile ones. As a result, hungan behavior is almost always to some extent aggressive. The aggression may remain confined to words.[14] If it turns physical, there are forms of ceremonial violence provided to dispel it: mock duels and the like. But simulated violence all too easily passes into the real thing;[15] and when it does, the possessed wield a strength more than human.[16]

But this is not the whole explanation of the possession-congregation's uneasiness. The possessed is not regarded simply as an unpredictable or violent man; he is not regarded simply as a man. In the eyes of those present, he *is* the god whom he incarnates[17] and, merely as such, dangerous beyond any physical danger. For he is one of those beings that "belong in some way to a different order of being, and therefore any contact with them will produce an upheaval at the ontological level which might well prove fatal."[18]

A clear sign of the uneasiness that possession-congregations feel toward a hungan is the effort many in the congregation make to avoid becoming possessed themselves. They employ certain talismans (bits of wax, knots in the hair, etc.) which are meant to block the spread of possession from one person to the next[19]—something which otherwise can occur at any moment,[20] and may continue until everyone on the scene has been infected.[21] The transmission may be by physical contact;[22] but it is not at all unusual for mere onlookers to be suddenly caught up in a trance.[23] Indeed, several possessions were reported among the audience of a *simulated* voodoo ceremony, performed at a 1966 Paris folk festival![24] One can understand an outsider's reluctance to be drawn into the psychic vortex of possession experience, but why should even worshippers in a possession cult fear possession? Again, there are practical reasons: for example, the fear of doing oneself or others violence while under the influence,[25] or the belief that accidental possession can result in sickness.[26] But again, the rational explanations are superficial ones. It is the possessed state *itself* that is feared, apart from any consequences that may result from it. For to be possessed is to relinquish, in greater or lesser degree, one's selfhood. Men flee it as they flee death because it *is* a kind of death. To be possessed is to die as an autonomous being, yet to keep on living without full consciousness or control: to become the "living dead." The way one dreads this as a fate for oneself is related to the dread one feels at the sight of those whose fate it has already become. Fear of the possessed, and of the actor insofar as he is possessed, must be understood as a response to the presence of the uncanny.

The uncanny would seem to be one of those affective states which is reducible to no category of feeling more basic than itself. However, in his essay *Das Unheimliche* Freud has found a way of "opening up" this seemingly irreducible emotion, and in so doing has provided a way of understanding the response of theatre audiences to the possessed actor.

Freud begins by noting, as had several writers before him, that a common feature of all uncanny phenomena is ambivalence: Does the vampire live or not? Must the house be looked upon as haunted or as just creaky? Is the fate of the temple violator curse or coincidence? According to Jentsch, this ambivalence is an intellectual uncertainty;[27] according to Wundt, it is a mixture of veneration and horror.[28] Freud sought an explanation at once more encompassing and truer to the feel of the experience itself than either of these.

He found an important clue in the German word for uncanny: *unheimlich*. *Unheimlich* is clearly formed as the negation of the adjective *heimlich* (alternate form: *heimisch*), meaning "native" or "familiar." But as Freud pursued the meanings of *heimlich* through Grimm's *Dictionary*, he found that the word can have meanings as diametrically opposed to its root-meaning as "secret," "hidden," and "withdrawn"; in fact, in some instances, "'*heimlich*' comes to have the meaning usually ascribed to '*unheimlich*.'"[29] This curious fact put Freud on the way to recognizing that "this uncanny is in reality nothing new or foreign, but something familiar and old-established in the mind that has been estranged only by the process of repression. . . . The *unheimlich* is what was once *heimisch*, home-like, familiar; the prefix '*un*' is the token of repression."[30]

But what are those feelings that have been repressed—and why have they been? Moreover, what is the quality common to all the experiences in which these feelings again become momentarily conscious in the form of a sensation of uncanniness? Freud answers these questions as follows:

> Let us take the uncanny in connection with . . . the return of the dead. The condition under which the feeling of uncanniness arises here is unmistakable. We—or our primitive forefathers—once believed in the possibility of these things and were convinced that they really happened. Nowadays we no longer believe in them, we have *surmounted* such ways of thought; but we do not feel quite sure of our new set of beliefs, and the old ones still exist within us ready to

seize upon any confirmation. As soon as something actually happens in our lives which seems to support the old, discarded beliefs we get a feeling of the uncanny; and it is as though we were making a judgement something like this: 'So, after all, it is true! . . . The dead do continue to live and appear before our eyes!'[31]

It would seem as though each one of us has been through a phase of individual development corresponding to that animistic stage in primitive men, that none of us has traversed it without preserving certain traces of it which can be reactivated, and that everything which now strikes us as 'uncanny' fulfills the condition of stirring those vestiges of animistic mental activity within us.[32]

It now becomes possible to see how Freud's theory of the uncanny accounts for the uncanniness of the performance event in general—an uncanniness that seems to arise irrespective of what the performance is about or what kind of performance it is (whether *Babes in Toyland* or *The Ghost Sonata*)—and for the uncanniness of the possessed actor in particular.

A performance as a whole is, as we saw in Chapter 1, precisely what Freud analyzes a manifestation of the uncanny as being: the *making present* of "vestiges of animistic mental activity" (or, as a more sympathetic writer might call them, "imaginative forms"). At theatre, too, we exclaim when suddenly faced with the presence of beings never before encountered outside the imagination: "So, then, it is true!" In fact, Freud's description of the ideal conditions for an experience of the uncanny:

An uncanny effect is often and easily produced by effacing the distinction between imagination and reality, such as when something that we have hitherto regarded as imaginary appears before us in reality.[33]

virtually coincides with the definition of a theatrical performance advanced in Chapter 1.

But our immediate concern is with the parallel between the ambivalent feelings produced in people by an experience of the uncanny and the responses aroused in them by the presence of the possessed actor. If a theatre performance is, as a whole, what Freud says the uncanny is—a sudden possibility of physical presence for imaginative conceptions—the possessed actor-hungan epitomizes this process in his own person. As the unfamiliar manifesting itself through the familiar; as a *heimlich* human form animated by *unheimlich* imaginative life; as a body "dead" to rational consciousness and being lived by repressed impulses—in all these ways the actor-hungan is a virtual living paradigm of the uncanny as Freud conceptualized it. And the ambivalent responses such a figure awakens in an audience—gratitude that he has made the Image present, together with mistrust of what he has become in the course of doing so—can best be understood as an instance of the *unheimlich-heimisch*.

As both the familiar and unfamiliar are present in the actor, both recognition and uneasiness are present in our response to him, but not in equal measure: uneasiness predominates. What ought to reassure us—the consideration that, however mysterious this figure may seem, he at least has a human body—is precisely what troubles us the most. The actor-hungan's human form only seems to underline how other-than-human this strange creature really is.

There are two further sources of our ambivalent but, on the whole, uneasy attitude toward the hungan-actor: (1) we do not know quite what to think of the beings he serves (the Images); and (2) we do not know quite what to think of him for serving them.

Our ambivalence toward Images themselves—an ambivalence which easily gets displaced onto the actor who embodies them—is a response to the quasi-sacred nature of those beings. Images are not gods, but they are eternal imaginative forms dwellings in an—if not THE—*illud tempus*; and as such, they elicit from us that strange blend of longing and terror which is the characteristic human response to anything numinous. Students of the classical languages have long been struck by the fact that the Latin word for "holy" (*sacer*) can also signify "accursed," and that the Greek *hagios* can mean either "pure" or "polluted."[34] What is behind this "self-contradictory attitude displayed by man in regard to all that is sacred"? Eliade offers the following explanation:

> On the one hand he hopes to secure and strengthen his own reality by the most fruitful contact he can attain with hierophanies . . . on the other, he fears he may lose it completely if he is totally lifted to a plane of being higher than his natural profane state.

> Resistance is most clearly expressed when a man is faced with a *total demand* from the sacred, when he is called upon to make the supreme decision—either to give himself over completely and irrevocably to sacred things, or to continue in an uncertain attitude towards them.[35]

Thus the Indian gods have each a gracious and a terrible aspect, and in the *Rig Veda* we find both prayers to be made one with Varuna and prayers to be delivered from him.[36]

Freud suggests that ambivalence toward noumena is the result of ambivalent feelings toward the human father, in whose image we have projected the noumena:

> It requires no great analytic insight to divine that God and the Devil were originally one and the same, a single figure which was later split into two opposed characteristics. . . .
> The antitheses contained in the original idea of the nature of God are but a reflection of the ambivalence governing the relation of an individual to his personal father.[37]

Similarly, he explains the taboo prohibition, that most rudimentary mode of the sacred, as a projection of unresolved ambivalence toward either the tabooed object itself or whatever the tabooed object has come to symbolize: an incestuous relationship, for example, which is both feared and desired.[38] (What need of prohibition if there were no evidence of desire?)

While all divinities are ambiguous figures, the possession gods to which theatre's Images can be likened have a reputation for being particularly so. The pantheon of the Nigerian *Bori* cult contains both good ("white") and evil ("black") deities, but each sort is capable of assuming the characteristics of the other.[39] The Dahomeans speak of saving themselves in spite of the *Voduns* (the local possession deities) by availing themselves of those same *Voduns'* powers.[40] Among the Alur, visitations of the possession god *Jok* "are greatly feared. Yet celebration and rejoicing to receive him are the only answer to his coming."[41]

Freud's theory explains not only the ambivalence felt toward gods in general, but also why this ambivalence should be particularly strong in the case of possession deities. As we saw in the last chapter,[42] a possession "god" is actually a socially acceptable form for the expression of repressed impulses. That the impulses in question have been *repressed* suggests why the gods who stand for them acquire a more than usual aura of ambivalence. Repression only occurs when a desire is felt so strongly that it cannot be acknowledged as being felt at all—that is to say, when an ambivalence reaches its extreme.

Thus, to the extent that Images are numinous, the insights of Eliade and Freud help to explain the ambivalence we feel toward them and (by contagion, as it were) toward the actors who embody them. Certainly Images present us with what Eliade calls a "total demand" that we abandon everyday criteria of the real and commit ourselves to their kind of reality—both a tempting and a disturbing proposition. And while Images, being elements in somebody else's imaginative projection, do not necessarily confront us with projections of our own ambivalences, the offer which they extend of participation in another's psychic life forces us into precisely the dilemma of Freud's savage before his taboo object: attracted (by the prospect of sharing in another's vision), yet terrified (that the price of this participation may be self-loss).

Even apart, then, from his own ambivalent status as one of the "living dead," the actor comes in for a share of that ambivalence which an audience is bound to feel toward the beings with whom he is so intimately connected. Eliade writes:

A king is an absolute powerhouse of forces simply because he *is* a king, and one must take certain precautions before approaching him; he must not be directly looked at or touched; nor must he be directly spoken to, and so on. In some areas the ruler must not touch the ground, for he has enough power in him to destroy it completely; he has to be carried, or to walk on carpets all the time. The precautions considered necessary when dealing with saints, priests and medicine men come from the same kind of fear.[43]

He might have included actors in his list. For they, too, become suffused with the terror of what they carry.

The other source of an audience's uneasiness with the actor-hungan is its feeling that he, in becoming the vehicle of the Image to which he was dispatched, has in a sense turned traitor.

The actor differs from other functionaries employed by society to go off and do something on its behalf in that, in order to fulfill the mission with which he has been entrusted, he must subvert it. The hunter departs in search of game and returns with game; the emissary is instructed to negotiate terms, and comes back with terms. But it was not to serve an Image as vehicle that the figure who eventually rounds back on us as the hungan-actor was sent forth. He was dispatched in the character of a shaman to bring us into the presence of some Image; but it is only by rounding, on the Image's behalf, back upon us that he can accomplish this task.

What can we know of Hamlet or Hedda Gabler, Webster's courts or Congreve's salons, Plautus and the bright world of the *Commedia*, unless we bid our actors make what the Catholic liturgy calls a "collect" of our need for and posture toward these *illa tempora*, and carry it out to that cleared circle where the Images await those through whom they will descend into our midst? Nevertheless, it is as much a betrayal as a fulfillment of this shamanic quest when the bearer of our "collect" *to* the Image transforms himself into an embodiment for us *of* the Image—that is, into a hungan. Our shaman-envoy to the Image went forth with us "behind him." But when the Image, to come among us, now chooses the same channel by which we invoked its descent—in other words, possesses itself of our envoy to serve as its embodiment—our envoy gives the impression of wheeling treacherously back on his old masters to confront them with the besought but terrifying presence of his new master, the Image. I have called this act a "rounding" because in it, as in a betrayal, our former envoy *faces about*. It is now the Image that "stands behind" him, where we once stood; and it is us, on whose behalf he had set out toward the Image, whom he now confronts—on the Image's behalf. He retains his character of envoy, but he has gone wholly from being our envoy to the Image to being the Image's envoy to us.

Of course a sense of betrayal is not the whole of an audience's response to the rounding. Once again we have to do with an ambivalence of feeling. If the actor-hungan has made rather free with his loyalties, his doing so has nonetheless brought us the presence of the Image we sought. Undeniably this strange event I have called the "rounding" manifests imaginative life in physical form; equally undeniably, it does so by inducing one among us to "change sides." The rounding thus has the dual character of epiphany and betrayal—epiphany ushered in by a treacherous act.

As epiphany, the rounding sharpens and clarifies perception. Regarding the hungans of Polynesia, Ellis writes that "the acts of the man during this period were considered as those of the god, and hence the greatest attention was paid to his expressions and the whole of his deportment."[44] So it is with our response to the actor-hungan, in whom is now present that presence we have longed to examine closely.

But in no lesser degree as betrayal, the rounding heightens perception. The betrayed have got to find out just how vulnerable the traitor's act has left them—and this means catching the exact purport of his every subsequent act and word. An audience which has been "rounded upon" by an actor pays him the same kind of attention a crowd pays one of its members who has just pulled a gun on the rest. Not so much curiosity about the Image, as healthy distrust of a man who has so lightheartedly betrayed his humanity to serve it, keeps them watchful.

In other words, *both* halves of the ambivalence generated in an audience by a "rounding" tend equally to increase audience perceptiveness: the element of epiphany, by producing reverent attention; the element of betrayal, by fostering nervous watchfulness. When we turn to the larger question of the group character of theatre audiences, we again find ambivalence of individual response serving, surprisingly, as a force for unity. The ambivalence each audience member feels toward the rounded, since all experience it, becomes the basis for a communality all can share: the common dilemma of having been rounded upon, with all the opportunities and dangers which that implies.

A group—any kind of group—tends toward singleness of response. Numberless experiments by social psychologists have shown that there is something about the mere fact of responding in the presence of other people that makes subjects respond more uniformly to a person or question than when each subject is tested by himself.[45]

Whether this tendency is cause for tears or rejoicing has long been a matter of controversy. Those pioneering students of group behavior, Le Bon and McDougall, saw the levelling as being all downward. According to Le Bon, group situations bring out the barbarian in even the most cultivated individual.[46] McDougall believed that in any given group the lowest intelligences drag all the others down to their level.[47] Gordon Allport, on the other hand, reached more ambiguous conclusions. He found that while the presence of others diminishes individual concentration and creativity, it also seems to increase the intensity and rate of mental processes.[48] And at the opposite extreme from Le Bon and McDougall, the experiments of Stoner suggest that group pressure actually drives individuals to make *more* audacious judgments than any one group member acting by himself would be likely to make.[49]

Whatever the direction of the levelling, a tendency toward uniformity of response in groups unquestionably exists. It is present even in groups whose members—like those of a theatre audience—are total strangers to one another.[50] It arises even in groups in which—again, as with theatre audiences—there is no opportunity for communication among the group members.[51] It seems that just the visible presence of a social context creates in individuals the need to be at one with it, and thereby with each other.[52] And where is "social context" ever more visibly present than in that veritable scale-model of social order, a theatre auditorium?

But what gives this trend toward uniformity a particular relevance to the case of theatre audiences is the fact that it operates most strongly in groups where ambivalence of feeling is the prevalent individual response:

> The general circumstances necessary for the . . . contagion of behavior . . . seem to be: . . . People must have two opposing impulses, the same two impulses for everyone. One of the impulses, the one initially dominant, is in conformity with a recognized norm or value, the other is not. The opposed impulses are such things as: . . . to make a confession . . . at a revival meeting, to remain . . . quiet.[53]

And most significant of all, the maximal conditions for uniform response occur in a group where there is not only ambivalent feeling but also a distinct leader at whom that ambivalence is directed: *precisely the situation obtaining between an audience and an actor-hungan.*

The emergence of a leader is the beginning of a collective character for the group he leads. An individual who separates off from a group to go forth and achieve something on its members' behalf confers upon that group the unity of a common relation to him. For example:

An individual separates off from us in order to govern us,

and *as against* this Ruler, we take on the collective character of The People.

An individual separates off from us in order to offer worship for us, and *as against* this Priest, we take on the collective character of The Congregation.

An individual separates off from us in order to perform theatre for us, and *as against* this Actor, we take on the collective character of The Audience.

Unity—at least unity of plight—is thus implicit in the very definition of an audience: those whom an actor, by going forth from their midst, has brought into the common situation of having been rounded upon. The rounding can— indeed, unless resisted for some of the reasons discussed in Chapter 6, the rounding *must*—coalesce even the most faction-ridden audience. The hostile individuals or groups within the audience cannot be so alien to each other as the hungan-actor, with his burden of nonhuman life, is to all of them. As the point from which all the others are equidistant, the actor serves as the center of a circle that joins them all. Audience unity is thus not a mystical goal, nor the by-product of some social or philosophical consensus which audiences in a fragmented society must despair of ever "achieving." It is *the nature of the event*, and theatre cannot be born without its being born.

What is the emotional basis for unity in a "led group" such as a theatre audience? In *Group Psychology and the Analysis of the Ego* Freud outlines the process of interaction between leader and group by which individuals' emotions become group feeling.

According to Freud, every ego contains a repressive, critical component, which he calls the "ego ideal."[54] In reality, this ego ideal is part of our own psyche; but when, as must often happen, we fail to meet its demands, we tend to project it outward onto somebody else whom we have a better chance of satisfying: say, a therapist or a lover. This "object" then "serves as a substitute for some unattained ego ideal of our own. We love it on account of the perfections which we have striven to reach for our own ego, and which we should now like to procure in this roundabout way as a means of satisfying our narcissism."[55]

A prime candidate to replace an individual's ego ideal under such circumstances is the leader of any group to which he may happen to belong. But if the members of a group *all* replace their respective ego ideals by the *same* group-leader, then they have, in effect, "identified with one another in their ego."[56] Such identification is the affective basis for communal feeling in a led group.

We can easily see how Freud's theory applies to a theatre audience. Each member of the audience has a desire for contact with the Image which, by himself, he is unable to gratify. Consequently, he replaces his own impulse toward the Image with the actor, who thus draws together all who have identified with him in this quest he has undertaken on behalf of all. Such identification is the affective basis for communal feeling in a theatre audience.

The surrender of an important function of the ego to another, be he actor, ruler, or priest, has, Freud points out, something regressive about it. It seems a reversion to the situation of the primal horde, where "the primal father is the group ideal which governs the ego in the place of the ego ideal."[57] Those who have achieved group feeling by such means stand in a relation to their leader in which "only a passive-masochistic attitude is possible."[58]

Now, while regressive passivity toward a leader is characteristic of any group, the effect is compounded in a theatre audience by those very aspects of the actor-audience relationship which I examined earlier in this chapter. The actor awakens regressive passivity in those for whom he performs, not just by virtue of his position as group-leader, but also because each of the ways in which actors make audiences uncomfortable—their being (as living dead) uncanny, their being intimately associated with noumena, their being "traitors"—further encourages a passive-regressive response.

Insofar as the actor is uncanny, he reawakens in the audience repressed childhood beliefs in the living dead and animism, and so encourages regression to the mentality of childhood.

Insofar as the actor is a "traitor," he produces in the audience feelings of powerlessness and vulnerability, and so returns them to the helpless passivity of the child.

And insofar as the actor is associated with noumena (the Images), he reactivates in the audience those childhood ambivalences toward the father, of which noumena are the projections.

The conclusion to which we seem driven is that the responses of theatre audiences are likely to be characterized by passiveness, ambivalence, and vulnerability. Are we to be dismayed by such a conclusion? That would be to miss the whole point! Passiveness, ambivalence, and vulnerability would be a dismaying combination of qualities in a parliamentary committee or a combat unit or a sports team. But what frame of mind did we expect would be induced in us by manifestations of an imaginative divine that call in question the most trusted ground-rule of our experience—the distinction between what is present and what is imagined? The passivity, etc., which theatre induces is the state of mind most favorable to its comprehension.

While this point is fresh might be a good moment to consider the phenomenon of audience participation.

Audience participation is the white hope of many who would give new life to the theatre. If only spectators could be got to talk to the actors, touch them, love them, and— *summum bonum*—undress with them, we would come marching into a new dawn; unresponsiveness would vanish; and theatre would once again engage the whole man as of yore.

In view of what I have shown the actor-audience relationship to be, this does not seem a very promising line of argument. I have pointed out that it is precisely by *depriving* us of the power to participate, by reducing us to the dilemma

of the crowd before the gunman, that the actor brings us
into being as the audience, the rounded upon. So long as
the actor was functioning as a shamanic voyager, we had at
least a vicariously active status: his voyage was to some
extent our voyage. But the first consequence of his transformation from shaman to hungan is our devolution from active
to helpless. For when the shaman rounds as hungan, he at
once withdraws the channel through which we had been able
to move out toward the Image, thus rendering us helpless,
and provides the Image with a channel for moving in toward
us, thus rendering us vulnerable. Awareness of this vulnerability is, as we have seen, the prime source of an audience's
attentiveness to theatre. How can those who would have us
shake it off imagine that they are helping us to be a better
audience?

Some probably suppose that in making theatre participatory, they are returning it to its pristine state. But in what
period has theatre ever been, for the audience, a place *to
do*? Others would like to see theatre more participatory
because they would like to see politics more participatory—
a type of analogy which I shall consider in Chapter 6.[59]

But in most cases it is not so much a positive ideal of
theatre as participatory, as dissatisfaction with a theatre
which is, among other things, nonparticipatory, that has
driven advocates of audience participation to their position. Their reasoning goes something like this: audiences
dread being made to participate, and ours is a dying theatre; free them from this inhibition about participating, and
our theatre will revive.

However, this "inhibition" is the most precious talisman
we possess for finding our way back to a genuine experience
of theatre, and he who would "free" me of it does me roughly the same service as one who would stamp out the single
ember by which I was trying to rekindle a fire. The dread
we feel at being asked to participate in the affairs of the
"rounded," far from establishing our deadness to theatre, is
the sure, joyful sign that some measure of susceptibility to its

Images has survived in us. Nothing could more eloquently witness to the power that these beings have upon our imagination than our shrinking involuntarily from their touch.

For what is it, after all, that lies behind the universal desire to be left alone when the "audience participation" starts? Is it embarrassment? Certainly that is a factor; no one wishes to be forced into prominence as the patsy of an accomplished, prepared, relaxed actor. But embarrassment simply does not account for the depth of our uneasiness as the actor draws closer—unless it be the embarrassment of human nature itself, at finding itself in the presence of the larger and more penetrating life of an embodied Image.

There is no justification for labelling the tendency to shrink from such encounters as "inhibition," "up-tightness," or whatever. On the contrary, it is those who think that they can get comfortable with noumena who are not facing the reality of their feelings. They are like the members of the repertory company in *Six Characters in Search of an Author:* at ease only because they have failed to recognize what they are in the presence of, too dumb to be scared. The fear of being introduced into a circle of demoniacs is not a barrier to be broken down so that theatre may impinge, but the glad evidence that it has never stopped impinging. This is the very fear by means of which the rounding brings the theatre into existence: fear of alien life, terrible even at the healthy distance of a cleared space.

For it would be misconstruing the whole situation to suppose that the actor only becomes intimidating when he invites participation; that so long as he keeps to his side of the footlights, he is not felt as posing a threat. Do you first fear the lion when he bursts his cage? Has your confidence that the lock would hold amounted to confidence in the lion? The discomfort that rises within us as the actor approaches our row, or the *chanteuse* our table, is but a more intense form, as strangeness draws closer, of the uneasiness which these rounded presences have already caused us from the stage. An actor in my lap is still an actor, as inexorably as if he held forth from the boards of the Comédie-Française. The intermingling or interseating of actors and audience—that wearisome experiment of Okhlopkov's which now, forty years later, is being hailed as the discovery of Grotowski and Richard Schechner—cannot bring the two groups an inch closer. What increase in rapport can be hoped from the physically nearer approach of beings who were never exactly in our space to begin with?

Some participationists have thought to unify cast and public by arranging for them to exchange, not positions, but roles: spectators are encouraged to *do*, actors to *look on*. Spectating and acting are thus conceived as being somewhat like the two ends of the Continental Railway: certain to meet, if only they are produced far enough into the area between. *But there is no "area between" spectating and acting.* Where the participationists have supposed a fascinating middle ground, there is only a sharp frontier. Actor and spectator are not, like male and female according to some psychologists, mere opposite directions along a gradually shading spectrum. To have rounded and to have been rounded upon are two different levels of reality. Theatre consists in the braving of each of these levels by the other; bring everyone onto a common level, and theatre has stopped being the case in that gathering. The participationists are right that there is nothing to prevent this from happening. A spectator can come forth from the audience and lay down his life to the Image, as the actors have done—thus becoming an actor. Or conversely, an actor can—though with difficulty, for as hungan he has forfeited full control of himself—reclaim his body from the Image and, in his own person, come over and socialize with the spectators (as in the recent New York production of *Tom Paine*)—thus joining the audience. In the former case you have an acting class; in the latter, a round-table discussion. In either case, you no longer have theatre; you have *changed the character of the assembly*.

Ultimately, then, the illusion that there is an "area between" spectating and acting is traceable to inadequate criteria for distinguishing theatre from other forms of activity. This distinction can be made on only one basis: Is the activity in question rounded—enactive of an Image—or not? And "rounded" or "not" are the only two possibilities. But within this distinction, too, participationists have managed to see a gray area, by confusing it with one of two other distinctions, each of which *does* contain a gray area.

In the first place, they have confused the distinction between what theatre is and what it is not with the distinction between what is tolerable to an audience and what is not—a distinction which everyone who works in theatre has an interest in testing, and which, moreover, certainly does contain a sizable gray area. The termini at either extreme are definite: an audience definitely *will* sit through an insult to their values, and just as definitely *will not* sit through being fired at with real bullets. But in between there is a wide spectrum of doubtful cases; for example: actor directs his insults to a particular woman in the fourth row (probably tolerable); actor throws apples at the audience (possibly tolerable); actor runs into audience and begins to punch individual spectators (probably intolerable). *However*, an action's verging toward or away from tolerability does not in the least imply its verging toward or away from being theatre. *All* the actions mentioned—from the insult to the fusillade—could be theatre *if performed by a rounded actor in the playing-out of his Image*.

"What! Even the real bullets?" This brings us to the second of the participationists' confusions: they mistakenly identify the distinction between what is theatre and what is not with the distinction between what is feigned and what is actually done. Once again, if the distinctions were equivalent, there would exist between theatre and "not-theatre" a considerable gray area: the realm of all those actions that lie between pretense and "meaning it." Between *those* alternatives, an actor clearly retains some leeway. He may drink the wine the script calls for or drink colored water, feign a slap or deliver it, brush his partner's lips or kiss her passionately on the mouth. But the extent to which the drinking, the slap, or the kiss is *theatre* in no way depends upon the extent to which it is feigned. *Both* the feigned and actual versions of each act can be theatre *if performed by a rounded actor in the playing-out of his Image.* Here, as so often, the psychology of ritual offers a helpful parallel. Among the Tikopia islanders of Polynesia,

> The numerous ceremonies that make up the periodical festivals—and which . . . are . . . only the reiteration of the paradigmatic acts of the gods—*seem* not to be different from normal activities: they comprise ritual repairing of boats, rites relative to the cultivation of food plants . . . repairing of sanctuaries. But in reality all these ceremonial activities differ from similar labors performed at ordinary times . . . because the ceremonies take place in an atmosphere saturated with the sacred. The natives, that is, are conscious that they are reproducing, to the smallest detail, the paradigmatic acts of the gods as they were performed *in illo tempore.*[60]

Similarly, the criterion of an action's being theatre is not the reality of the action but the state of mind of the person who performs it; that is, whether he regards it as his deed or the Image's. Two stagehands fooling with prop swords is not theatre, though it is feigning. Hotspur's and Hal's duel is theatre, though the actors were to bare their swords' points. In the late Roman theatre a death called for by the script was sometimes actually inflicted, the actor involved being a felon due for execution anyway.[61] This goes beyond decency, but does not necessarily go beyond the definition of theatre, any more than does a real onstage slap or kiss. (Of course, it can hardly have been very good theatre; such "actors" must have been too preoccupied for their Images to take hold.)

In the earlier sections of this chapter I showed that several kinds of ambivalence characterize the figure of the actor and, consequently, the nature of an audience's response to him.

There is a story about a performance of *Othello* at which a spectator, in order to forestall any further treachery from Iago, shot dead the actor who was playing him.[62] This is no more than a particularly vivid instance of the refusal on the part of participationists to acknowledge such ambivalences. Insofar as they treat the actor as just another human being to relate to, they are refusing to acknowledge how carefully poised this figure is between the human and the numinous, the envoy and the traitor, the living and the dead. And insofar as they claim to feel nothing in the presence of actors but mutuality and warmth, they are refusing to acknowledge how uncomfortable an experience it is to be rounded upon.

But these ambivalences refused by the participationist are not just an incidental side-effect of theatre; they arise from the very nature of the theatrical event. How could theatre be an experiment in commingling irreconcilable modes of truth—the imaginative and the present—and not impart a certain ambiguity to those figures in whom the irreconcilables meet? How could theatre *be* an ambivalence and not *evoke* ambivalence?

Consequently, in refusing these ambivalences, what the participationists are really refusing is the theatrical event itself. Their secret wish is to bypass the incarnatory process by which theatre makes imaginative forms present and go directly into the presence of . . .

But of what?

Of actors? But how can they be actors if they have been relieved of the burden of the Image?

Of Images? But with the actors reabsorbed into the human midst, there is no way for any Images to be present.

Thus, under the pressure of attempts at audience participation, the theatre splits apart into a physical life without imaginative dimension and an imaginative life incapable of presence—that is to say, assumes the form of that very rift between imagination and presence which characterizes our experience in the absence of theatre, and which theatre specifically addresses itself to healing. Audience participation, in seeming to provide a way of drawing nearer to the theatrical event, in fact abolishes it.

Those who advocate audience participation show evidence of a right instinct gone astray. The right instinct is the need they feel to increase the number of levels on which audiences can participate in theatre. Where it goes astray is in their supposing the literal sense of "participate"—take a part, go onstage, touch, do—to be among those levels. They mistake what is really an impulse to bring more of oneself into play for a directive to bring oneself more into the play.

Theatre, a complex score of emotional, formal, rhythmic, sensory, and conceptual elements, indeed demands participation on every level we are capable of. For most theatregoers, however, participation in the theatre has shrunk to one out of all these possible levels: empathic "involvement" in the fortunes of characters. With such spectators it tends to be the case that, when there is nothing going on for them to "get involved" in, there is, quite simply, nothing going on for them. As one mode of awareness among others, empathic feeling is a tolerable—and probably an inevitable—response to theatre. But too exclusive a concern for the perils of Pauline may narrow awareness of those expressive resources by which alone either Pauline or her perils become present to empathize with.

However, to recognize that theatre demands more than empathic response is not to pronounce it participatory. The way we "participate" in a work of art is by being the audience among whom its fullness is possible; and the levels on which an obsession with empathy keeps audiences from responding are all levels of *perception*. In a word, what theatre-goers need to participate in is an awareness—a layered awareness of how the *illud tempus* manifests itself at once through actors' bodies, scenic resources, and language. (We have already considered the share of the actor in this process; in the two following chapters we will examine the manifestory roles of scenic expression and dramatic language, respectively.) All an audience can "do" in the theatre falls into the category of what it can do for its own responsiveness to these elements. More, however, can be achieved along these lines than is generally realized.

My concern here is not primarily with questions of theatre education. But participationist practices are so often defended on the grounds of their educational value—they are said to deepen engagement, heighten response, and so forth—that I feel, having denied any such value to them, an obligation to suggest some alternate method of audience education, free from participationist confusions.

Since the role of the audience in theatre is a perceptual one, any program of audience education must first and foremost seek to develop the requisite perceptual abilities. I shall describe two techniques by which I believe this can be accomplished: *perception exercises* and *audience rehearsals.*

In the kind of perception exercise I have in mind, a single element of dramatic expression would be selected to vary—all other elements being held constant—through several consecutive stagings of the same short scene or pantomime. By noting how successive changes in that one element were altering the net effect of the scene from version to version, the audience would come to realize what expressive contributions that element is capable of making to the theatrical event.

For example, in a blocking exercise the pattern of movement might, in successive stagings, first reinforce, then qualify, then undercut the pattern of interaction implied by the script. In an exercise on the functions of light, lighting could be used first to create a sense of place, then to suggest character relationships, then to underline one character's experience of the scene. The expressive effects of stage space could be demonstrated by playing the same scene first on a bare stage, then on a realistic setting, then on a schematic simplification of that setting. And so forth.

A cycle of such exercises, spread over several evenings and taking up each of the basic resources of the stage in turn—at first singly, then perhaps in combinations of two or more—would constitute an introductory course in theatrical expression, comparable to those slide-lectures and piano-demonstrations by which the rudiments of art and music are now taught. One can think of several institutional contexts in which such a course might be welcome. It would make a vivid supplement to a college program in dramatic literature or criticism. It could be presented by a local repertory company as part of a program of "audience development" (a phrase at present understood by these groups as referring solely to the enlargement of their subscription lists). It could figure in the adult education curriculum of a community center or in a university extension program. The technical demands would, for the most part, be nothing beyond what most high school and civic auditoriums can provide.

The other technique of theatre education which I should like to propose is the *audience rehearsal*. By this I do not mean either audiences watching actors rehearse or members of the audience themselves rehearsing for subsequent participation. (Proposals for both these kinds of "audience rehearsal," incidentally, were under discussion in the early twentieth-century Russian theatre.)[63] Rehearsal is the time to work on the contribution *you* are going to make to the theatrical event; and if you are a member of the audience, that means your perceptiveness. What I mean by an audience rehearsal is an opportunity for those who will be the eventual spectators of a given production to increase their capacity for the kinds of perceptivity which that production will require of them.

A cycle of audience rehearsals would therefore be very like the cycle of perception exercises I have just outlined, except that exercises would be chosen with a view to meeting the particular perceptual demands of the production in question. In audience rehearsals of *The Three Sisters*, for example, the emphasis would be on exercises that increase

responsiveness to such expressive devices as the use of
action on one part of the stage as a comment on action elsewhere; the expression of dramatic relationships through
color relationships; the employment of commonplace events
as stage-metaphors.

Audience rehearsals, though they would be separate from
(and probably less frequent than) actors' rehearsals, would
nonetheless be carefully coordinated with them. Most likely,
the audience rehearsals would have a leader of their own,
though it is conceivable that the leader of the actors' rehearsals (i. e., the director of the production) might want to
run both rehearsal cycles. But whether or not they were pre-
sided over by the same leader, the exercises that the audience witnessed would be performed not only by the same
actors they were preparing to see perform the play, but
(ideally) in the same theatre and on the very sets to be used
in performance. The schedules of the cast and audience rehearsals would be synchronized so that both groups could
feel that they were exploring the same aspect of the play
at the same time. Thus, as the cast uncovered, say, parallel
relationships, it would pass its discoveries on to the audience
in the form of exercises showing how blocking and costume
can underline such parallels.

It is admittedly difficult to think of an existing institutional context in which audience rehearsals might take place;
though here again, the university drama course might provide a point of departure. But if the audience rehearsal is a
somewhat utopian suggestion on the institutional level, it has
at least the merit—unlike the programs of the participationists
—of being realistic about the kind of event theatre is. Indeed,
it would constitute true audience participation; for opening
night would come as the climax of the collective efforts
of the troupe and the audience that had worked in tandem
with them to create the ideal perceptual conditions for their
performance. (Perhaps there would only *be* an opening
night: such a production could exist in its fullness only be-

fore those who had given themselves to the collaboration.) For once, "rounded" and "rounded upon" would have joined forces in the service of—without at the same time attempting to dispel that mutual tension which is the essence of—the theatrical event.

CHAPTER 4

The Scenic Means

By "scenic means" I refer primarily to stage space, scenery (both two-dimensional and three-dimensional), blocking, and light.

Though it may seem rather late in the day to be asking this: Why should theatre want—or, granted that it wants, why should it be entitled to—means of expression so different from, and (one might suppose) so incompatible with, one another as these? We are too apt to take for granted that theatre should just have everything at its disposal. Even minimalists like Copeau and Grotowski feel that they are foregoing what is theirs to forego. But why, when painting must make do with visual effect, and dance with movement, and music with sound, should theatre be able to count visual effect, movement, and sound all equally among its resources? And why, when new expressive modes are invented (film, electric light, recording) is theatre universally conceded the right to acquire them? Of course, many playwrights, directors, and designers would deny that some one (or all) of these elements belong in the theatre. But even the significance of this denial cannot be understood until one has grasped what role the scenic means can legitimately be thought of as playing in the theatrical event. I therefore defer consideration of the campaign for bare stages until the end of this

chapter, and, plunging into the subject from quite the opposite direction, I shall start by considering the moment in
Western theatrical history when scenic expression showed its
first signs of independent development as a prominent, even
central, aspect of the theatrical event. The circumstances of
this historical development provide a valuable clue as to why
theatre should ever have developed a scenic dimension at all.

Though ultimately to achieve its most characteristic suc-
cesses in production styles that are far from illusionistic,
scenic expression began to come into its own at the moment
when Western theatre first began to prize illusionism as a
performance value. If one had to guess when that moment
occurred, one would probably say: with the advent of naturalism. It is true that illusionistic stagecraft was essential to
the productions of an Antoine or a Stanislavski. But the scenic
techniques of which the naturalists availed themselves pre-
date that movement by several centuries and were developed
in the service of a theatre form diametrically opposed to
naturalism: the Renaissance intermezzo, as performed in the
courts of Italy, and those French and English descendants
of the intermezzo (at least as far as scenic method is concerned), the baroque opera and the masque. (Since it is the
scenic features common to the intermezzo, baroque opera,
and the masque that concern me, I shall, unless otherwise
specified, use the term "intermezzo" to cover all three.)
As a rule intermezzi depicted events of a fabulous, not
to say phantasmagoric, nature. So we are faced with a seeming paradox: realism of scenic depiction first arose in a theatre that, insofar as subject matter was concerned, cared
nothing for reality. In this seemingly paradoxical relation
between the subject matter and the scenic mode of the intermezzo lies the key to the entire role of scenic means in the
theatre.

Whether performed at tourneys, at balls, or between the
acts of a play,[1] the short but elaborate spectacles known to

the Italians as "intermezzi" had always one thing in common: subject matter that was fanciful in the extreme. A production number featuring a sea nymph accompanied by dolphins and Tritons might alternate with a battle between Apollo and a dragon. Gods descended, heavens opened, demons strove; and the scene shifted between such locales as Constantinople, the palace of the sun, and a sorcerer's cave.[2]

The scenic methods of showing these strange events were as realistic as ingenuity could make them—as realistic, one might say, as the events themselves were unreal. A scenography textbook of the period like Sabbattini's *Manual for Constructing Theatrical Scenes and Machines* (1638)[3] contains numerous suggestions on how to simulate real phenomena: fires, storms, gradually darkening skies. But it is clear that what really interested Sabbattini were realistic methods of showing utterly fantastic events: the sudden appearance of a Hell or Paradise; the transformation of a man into a rock or of a rock into a man. It almost seems as if the stranger the event, the more complete had to be the scenic realism with which it was managed.

The most frequent and (in that it usually came as the climax) most conspicuous of all these unreal but realistically rendered intermezzo-events was the descent of a divine or mythical world onto the stage. That is, intermezzi tended to be *about* the event which all theatre *is*: the manifestation of an *illud tempus* in human surroundings.

The nature of these divine or mythical worlds varied considerably—which, again, might be said of theatre itself, with its plurality of script *illa tempora*. What descended might be a mere temple full of mythological statues[4] or an actual assembly of the gods.[5] It might be the golden age of classical mythology[6] or a golden age of imaginative achievement (as when Chaucer, Spenser, Lydgate, and Gower are manifested at the climax of one of Ben Jonson's masques).[7] Or it might be, quite simply, Paradise,[8] the methods of depicting which Sabbattini discusses in some detail.[9] But the most striking parallel between one of these intermezzo-descents and the basic theatrical event itself occurs in Jonson's *Hymenaei*:

> No less to be admired for the grace and greatness was the whole machine of the spectacle, from which [the female masquers] came, the first part of which was a *mikrokosmos*, or globe, filled with countries, and those gilded; where the sea was expressed, heightened with silver waves.[10]

What is performance itself but the eruption of just such a *mikrokosmos*—a perennial *illud tempus*, full of eternal inhabitants—into our midst?

But it is not only in their plot-events that the intermezzi reflect a preoccupation with the process of manifestation. The resources of scenic expression themselves, which are our present concern, are products of the same preoccupation. This is not merely to say that ways of bringing gods and spirits onto the stage had to be (and were) found.[11] I mean that the very devices of Renaissance scenic art owe their existence, not so much to an appetite for realism as such, but to a desire *to show in visual form the process of manifestation which is theatre*. I shall take three of these devices—instantly changing sets, perspective scene-painting, and the *scena ductilis*—and show how each contributed to make the intermezzo-stage a model in space of the theatrical event.

"The disappearance and changing of scenes," writes Sabbattini, "is a thing which ordinarily arouses great delight and wonder among the spectators, particularly when the change is made so quickly that no one notices it";[12] and his textbook includes advice on "How to Stage the Total Destruction of the Scene"[13] and "How to Darken the Whole Scene in a Moment."[14] One might be tempted to write off this fascination with instant set-changes as indicating nothing more than a taste for gimmickry. But the terms in which contemporary spectators described their experience of these effects suggests a deeper level of engagement. The aim of such effects was to "make the spectators themselves see a thing which they denied could be done."[15] That aim was certainly achieved in the case of one spectator, who wrote afterwards: "The grandeur of the spectacle cannot be told; he who did not actually see it must fail to credit its wonders."[16] This is the language in which a person speaks of a miracle. That we cannot be sure whether the miracle was felt to consist in the mythic events portrayed or in the scenic means of portraying them is a significant ambiguity. It is as if the miraculousness of the theatre technology was perceived as a kind of stage-equivalent for the miraculousness of the event itself.

What is there about quick changes of scene that they should be capable of eliciting such response? Elsewhere than in the theatre, the experience of place A is invariably linked to the experience of place B by a third experience: that of getting from A to B, so that neoclassical critics can hardly be blamed for having wondered how theatre produces the effect of A-then-B without going anywhere. It is only consenting to discuss the question in sterile categories to reply: "Imagination has wings." Change of place is accomplished in the theatre without the benefit of *any* locomotion, winged or otherwise. An Image, in manifesting itself, brings its world along with it, just the way a traveller, stepping into a restaurant out of a blizzard, carries the storm into the diners' midst. A change of place occurs in the theatre when Image A vanishes, taking its space with it, and Image B manifests itself, bringing *its* space along. Thus fascination with changes of scene in the theatre is in fact fascination with the course of the Image's transit, that is, with the process of manifestation itself.

Perspective scene-painting—another design technique employed for the first time in the intermezzo—puts the eye through a kind of perceptual equivalent of the actor's relations with the *illud tempus*. The vanishing point in a perspective painting is perceived either as a goal toward which the space pouring into the picture from all sides converges [17] (*Diagram 1A*), or as the source from which all space in the picture flows out (*Diagram 1B*). These two possibilities parallel the two directions of an actor's passage between our world and the *illud tempus*. Insofar as the spectator's eye is drawn in *toward* the vanishing point, there is perceptual reenactment of the shaman-actor's going forth to the *illud tempus*. Insofar as the scene is perceived as flowing out *from* the vanishing point to fill the spectator's field of vision, there is perceptual reenactment of the Image's coming forth (with the aid of the hungan-actor) from the *illud tempus* into our midst.

A.
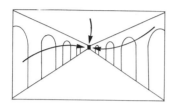
B.
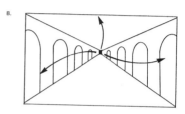

C.
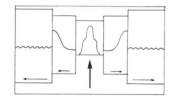
D.
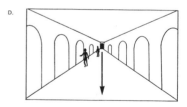

Diagram 1: Renaissance perspective scenery and the journey to/from the *illud tempus*. *Drawing by Anne Geer.*

The *scena ductilis*, another scenic device developed for use in the intermezzi, made happen on stage what perspective scenery made happen in the perceptual field of the observer: it conducted the eye on a gradual, shamanlike penetration of the (intermezzo's) *illud tempus*. The *scena ductilis* consisted of a series of paired flats, the frontmost pair of which provided the initial backdrop, until its two halves were drawn apart to reveal the next paired-flat back-drop, and so on, for as many drops as there were episodes[18] (*Diagram 1C*). The sense of distinct, successive stages of penetration into an *illud tempus* which this device must have produced is analogous to the following shamanic practice, particularly in view of the fact that what the final pair of flats often parted to reveal was heaven: "The Altaic shaman ritually climbs a birch tree in which a certain number of steps have been cut . . . the steps representing the various heavens through which the shaman must pass on his ecstatic journey to the highest heaven."[19] (One thinks, too, of all those "ladders of perfection" and terraced spiritual mountains in the writings of the mystics.)[20] When the final pair of flats had parted, then, "from the depths of this image of order,"[21] the inhabitants of the now penetrated-to *illud tempus* (the courtly masquers) began their move outward toward the audience (*Diagram 1D*). This outward procession of the masquers makes an explicit stage event of the hunganic phase of manifestation (the procession of embodied Images into our midst), even as the successively opening flats of the *scena ductilis* had made an explicit stage event of the earlier, shamanic phase.

What general conclusion concerning the function of scenic representation in the theatre can be drawn from this brief account of the Renaissance intermezzo? The scenic devices first came into prominence in the service of a theatre form which takes as its subject matter the basic process of an actor's work: manifestation of an *illud tempus*. What is more, the devices themselves—scene-changing machines, perspective scenery, the *scena ductilis*—demonstrate aspects of this very process. *Surely behind the compulsion to* depict *the process lies a yearning to* share *in it*. But what share can nonhuman elements have in the (as it has thus far appeared) uniquely human transaction between an actor, an Image, and an audience?

The manifestation of a numinous presence in and through a physical thing, Mircea Eliade calls a "hierophany."[22] Till now, the only object we have considered as a possible vehicle for hierophany is the body of the hungan-actor, in and through which the presence of the numinous Image is manifested. But theatre is an instrumentality for "making presence," and as such, it must have ways of handling all the ways an event has of *being* present: not only as human interchange, but as spatial arrangement, as color pattern, as sequence of movements, and so forth. These aspects of presence can, for the most part, be manifested only by such nonhuman vehicles as space, setting, blocking configurations, and light. The scenic means find a place in the theatre because they can become hierophanies in instances where the human body cannot.

Indeed, it is inherent in the concept of a hierophany that *any* thing can become one:

> We cannot be sure that there is *anything*—object, movement, psychological function, being, or even game—that has not at some time in human history been somewhere transformed into a hierophany. It is a very different matter to find out *why* that particular thing should have become a hierophany, or should have stopped being one at any given moment. But it is quite certain that anything man has ever handled, felt, come in contact with or loved *can* become a hierophany.[23]

To the extent that in a hierophany the vehicle "becomes *something else*, yet . . . continues to remain *itself*,"[24] we may even speak (loosely, to be sure) of a physical object as "rounding"—indeed, as rounding with, if anything, even more readiness than a person. As the Image approaches with its demands, even the most experienced hungan-actor still has to contend with the instinct to protect his body against usurpation, whereas an object, will-less and passive, makes no resistance to being caught up into the life of an *illud tempus*. This is why a prop can be of so much help to an actor in getting into a difficult role. The prop can pass effortlessly across the gulf he is having trouble maneuvering, and perhaps show him a passage.

A proof that objects can become instinct with the life of the *illud tempus* is the uneasiness which a prop can still inspire after the performance, just as if it were a human actor—and for the same reason. Once an object has been used in the *Bori* possession ritual, it is believed to retain certain properties ever after (for example, the power to cause impotence or repel witches) and "becomes invested with a halo of fear and respect."[25] Similarly, a knife once used onstage to commit a murder (or for that matter, a racket once used onstage to play tennis) cannot go back to being just one more item in the property collection. To it, as to the actor back in his dressing-room, a taint of numinous affiliation still clings.

It is possible to explain the presence in theatre of each of the scenic resources in terms of the particular aspect of the *illud tempus* (or, in some cases, of the Image itself) which that resource, being particularly well qualified to manifest, is entrusted with manifesting. In fact, it is not only possible, it is necessary to account for the presence of each of these resources in this way. For unless an expressive resource can have a role in making the *illud tempus* present, it cannot have a role in theatre, which is nothing but the making present of an *illud tempus*. Let us see what aspect of the *illud tempus* each of the principal scenic resources—stage space, scenery, blocking, and light—is particularly well suited to serve as the hierophany of.

Stage Space. Theatre does not simply occur in available space the way a boat-ride occurs in a lake. Theatre must create its own space, like a tunnelling animal. Most of the elements of theatre have a role to play in clearing, shaping, and delimiting this space. But the *source* of the space that all these elements work on, the source of the very possibility of space in the theatre, is the possessed body of the actor.

Any "irruption of the sacred . . . results in detaching a territory from the surrounding cosmic milieu and making it qualitatively different."[26] For "when the sacred manifests itself in any hierophany, there is . . . a break in the homogeneity of space" occasioned by the "revelation of an absolute reality, opposed to the nonreality of the vast surrounding expanse."[27]

The possessed hungan-actor has this detaching, "sacralizing" effect—detaching *by* sacralizing—on the site he chooses for his "irruption" into our midst. Stage space is the physicalization of the "rounded" actor's apartness, which I considered in the last chapter: the distant*ness* become distance. It is the spatial symptom of the psychic gap which one who serves noumena opens out between the rest of us and himself. It is the extent of an uneasiness.

Consequently, the dimensions and shape of a playing area are determined by where the actors take up their positions. For since stage space is the spatialization of the actor's otherness, its contours depend entirely on the distance over which he is able to make that otherness felt.

Blocking. Any manifesting an actor accomplishes through his own movements and gestures belongs to the hierophany of the possessed body of the actor, not to the category of scenic means. But the pattern of several actors' movements are hierophanic in a way that a single moving body cannot be.

Blocking, the pattern plotted by actors' movements, manifests human relationships as visual patterns. The nature of these patterns reveals the kind of *illud tempus* from which the Image in question proceeds, by displaying the kind of relationships it is possible for people to move into there.

Consider, for example, this bit of symbolic blocking from the mediaeval rite of the Mass:

> The movement of the bishop to the right side of the altar is, by positional symbolism, a movement toward paradise, hence, a re-enactment of the Resurrection. Meanwhile, the deacons stand between him and the congregation, three on the left and four on the right, representing the Old and New Testaments and also the readiness of the disciples to follow Christ even to death.[28]

The blocking having thus revealed physical space to be the

dimension of redemptive change, we know we are in the world of spiritual action.

Of course, since that is where we expect to be in almost any ritual, we may not be especially conscious of having had the nature of a world revealed to us. But in theatre different kinds of stage-worlds are possible, and we must rely on blocking to show us which kind is present on a particular occasion. For blocking can reveal things about a space which the space would be incapable of revealing about itself.

For example, if distances, tensions, and approaches in the blocking occur at moments of emotional distance, tension, and approach in the action, then the world implied is one of psychological relations.

If the blocking shows a frightened adolescent, center, surrounded by an arc of authority figures (teacher, parent, general, priest), then the world implied is the inner space of the central character's mind, for that is the only place where all such characters configure in that way.

If the blocking shows three men, all of whom are supposed to be watching the same event, looking one to the right, one out, and one over his head, then the implied world is a relativistic one, where every man's plane of perception contradicts every other's, and none can claim absolute validity.

If the blocking shows an actor struggling in waves, dragging himself onto an island and hailing a passing ship, and if island, waves, and ship are all composed of other actors, then what is being implied is a world which human action creates—or, more grandly, that human action creates the world.

It seems we must make an exception in the case of realistic blocking, which only attempts to transcribe the look of the world as given. For in the world as given, people's movements do not always, or even often, manifest the truth of their relationships. But blocking which cannot be trusted to manifest relationships implies a world as definitely as any other kind of blocking: a world in which spiritual and psychological forces do not become physically manifest. Just phrasing it that way, however, brings out the inherent contradiction between realistic blocking and the nature of theatre. For theatre is the place where manifestness *is* attained (by the Image), the place where the look of things invariably *does* imply the truth of their nature. The sort of realistic blocking where movement seems to be now mere locomotion, now the externalization of emotional pattern, represents the kind of compromise realistic theatre is obliged to make between the conflicting demands of realism and theatre.

Scenery. Scenery is the hierophany of context. That is, scenery manifests whatever it is, back in the *illud tempus*, that must be thought of as either physically surrounding or thematically "going with" the Image.

Most religions regard their ritual sites as replicas of some divine original in the *illud tempus.* When Solomon declared the altar he was building to be "a resemblance of the holy tabernacle which Thou hast prepared from the beginning,"[29] he was giving voice to a belief almost universal in ancient and primitive societies.[30] In those possession religions which we have so often had occasion to compare with theatre, this belief acquires particular urgency. For in *their* ritual places the god may actually *appear*, and if he does so, he will expect to find himself in familiar surroundings. For this reason the Yoruba of Brazil, though exiled to the New World, still construct their ceremonial grounds on the model of an African village; for their gods dwell in the *illud tempus* of an eternal, mystical "Africa," and only where "Africa" has been made present can they be made present.[31] Such is the perspective in which a set designer should view his work: as the making present of whatever site in the *illud tempus* must accompany the Image if it is to come among us.

This is not, of course, meant as an endorsement of any particular style of stage design. But it does provide a basis for resolving one of the most persistent problems in design aesthetics. Many—notably Craig and Appia—have held the juxtaposition onstage of solid objects and painted representations of objects to be an incongruity. In fact, however, such juxtapositions are perceived not only as coherent but as expressive of something crucial about the Image.

Think of the impression we receive when we look simultaneously at the protruding tip and underwater base of a sea rock. The tip, jutting out into the air, has fully made the transit from underwater and become an object in our world; the undersea base has remained behind in another, (from our point of view) less actualized and basically two-dimensional world: the shadowy depths as viewed through the glassy surface. And yet, despite this visual disparity, we perceive tip and base as participating in a common being, that of the rock as a whole, whose less and more fully realized aspects are, it never occurs to us to doubt, continuous with each other.

So it is with painted and solid objects on a stage: they are perceived as, respectively, the less and more fully realized aspects of the *illud tempus*. If the three-dimensionality of certain objects is a sign of their having "made it across" with the Image when the Image made its transit into our world, the two-dimensionality of other, painted objects is a reminder that there are elements of the *illud tempus* that remain behind, but which could be present any time the Image might feel the need of them. We *want* to be able to show distinct degrees of "manifestness." To be able to suggest what is inseparable from an Image and what, though related, is only incidental to it, is an expressive resource.

Light. That color relationships can externalize dramatic relationships, that different illuminations can give the same scene different meanings—these are important extensions of light's role in the work of manifestation. But the very *presence* of light in the theatre, the sheer white fact of it, is attributable to the effects of possession by an Image on the body of an actor.

As light is almost everywhere considered an attribute of divinity, numinous figures are almost always thought of as irradiating light. Buddha appears as a column of fire.[32] Krishna reveals himself as "shiningly effulgent . . . blazing all around like the burning fire . . . dazzling to the sight."[33] The features of the transfigured Christ "shine as the sun"; his garments are "white as the light."[34]

Not only actual gods but, more to our purpose in considering the relation between light and the actor, human beings *close* to the gods become sources of illumination. Sri Ramakrishna seemed to his disciples to be "surrounded by flames."[35] Zarathustra while still in his mother's womb gave forth radiance enough to light a whole village.[36] When Saint Seraphim of Sarov addressed his followers, it was like "the face of a man speaking to you from the middle of the sun."[37]

Both the power to emit light and the tendency to suffuse the human body with it are specifically attributed to possession deities. The Somali *jinns* appear in the form of uncanny nocturnal flashes and will-o'-the-wisps.[38] The Dinka possession god "Flesh" manifests himself in a red light. A hymn in his honor which begins: "The Flesh kindles like fire"[39] summarizes the connection I would argue exists between the body of the possessed actor and stage light.

Contact with the *illud tempus* sets the human figure aglow; for, in the words of a fourteenth-century theologian, "he who shares the divine energy . . . becomes himself in some sort light."[40] Thus when Moses came down off Mount Sinai, "the skin of his face shone."[41] It is significant that so long as he remained in this state, "the children of Israel . . . were afraid to come nigh him."[42] For, while Moses was not possessed, the connection between the uneasiness he inspired and the light he gave off reveals a parallel with the hungan-actor. The rounding invests the man who undergoes it with distantness and strangeness. If stage space

physicalizes the distantness as distance, stage light physicalizes the strangeness as aura. And since "distantness" and
"strangeness" are really only two different metaphors for the
essential otherness of the "rounded" actor, the lighted area
that surrounds him is exactly coterminous with the space he
has, in rounding, opened out around himself. The tapering
off òf this light's intensity in all directions out from him manifests, as do the limits of the playing area, the decrease in aura
of an uncanny figure, the more distance you succeed in putting between yourself and him.

If the scenic resources in general can best be understood
as means of hierophany, specific conventions of stage and
theatre construction in particular periods can often best be
understood as attempts to have the very look of the theatre-
site illustrate the process of hierophany that occurs there. I
do not claim to be able to account for the structure of every
theatre the world has ever known in these terms. I confine
myself to four—all, however, central and significant—styles
of theatre construction: the Japanese Noh stage, the classical Greek stage, the Elizabethan public playhouse, and the
post-Renaissance proscenium auditorium. And even in these
cases, I am more interested in drawing a few suggestive analogies than in elaborating a comprehensive theory.

Of all the theatre traditions which now exist, or perhaps
have ever existed, the Noh theatre of Japan is the most forth-
right in acknowledging its nature as manifestation. What we
have seen is implicit in all theatre becomes explicit in Noh.
The shamanic inner voyage that all actors make, the Noh
actor *looks* like he is making; he seems, wrote Yeats, "to re-
cede from us into some more powerful life . . . he receded,
but to inhabit as it were the deeps of the mind."[43] If all
actors are possessed by their Images in a sense, the Noh actor
is believed to be possessed by his Image in actual fact.[44]
And to an even greater degree than with the Renaissance
intermezzo, the scripts (at least those of the most performed

"Noh of Spirits") have hierophany as their chief subject
matter: the apparition of a dead gardener to the girl who
rejected him,[45] the manifestation of a mountain goddess to
a party of climbers,[46] and so forth. The source of dramatic
interest at a Noh performance is explicitly recognized to be
what, in fact, it is at any theatrical event: "the suspense of
waiting for a supernatural manifestation—which comes."[47]
But most significant for our present purpose, practically
every detail of the highly conventionalized Noh stage (*Diagram 2*) is designed to keep before the spectator's mind some
aspect of the actor's work of manifestation.

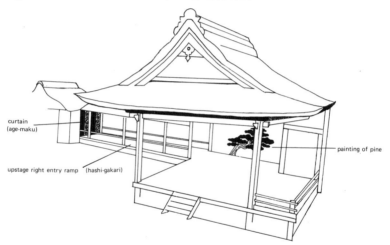

Diagram 2: The Japanese Noh stage. *Drawing by Anne
Geer.*

The Noh stage is approached by a long, flat ramp
(*hashi-gakari*), upstage right. Each actor makes his initial
appearance through a curtain (*age-maku*) at the far end of
this ramp, then slowly passes across the ramp onto the
stage.[48] Both curtain and ramp are visual reminders of
shamanic-hunganic transit.

The drawing of the curtain to reveal the actor symbolizes
the drawing aside of the veil which, until the actor makes
them visible by embodying them, conceals the Images from

our view. This symbolism also, of course, attaches to the raising or parting of curtains in our Western proscenium theatres.

The ramp, which Pound thought contained "no special symbolism,"[49] in fact symbolizes the very possibility of the manifestational process. Cultures as diverse as the Persian and the Finnish have the myth of a narrow bridge joining our world to the *illud tempus*.[50] Most men cross this bridge only after death, but shamans possess the ability not only to cross it while still alive (in moments of trance), but also to find their way back across it to the world of men.[51] Clearly, the "narrow bridge" is a symbol of the shaman's skill in voyaging between our world and the *illud tempus*; and the presence of an actual narrow bridge giving entry to the Noh stage shows an explicit recognition that such transits are accomplished there as well. The same symbolism attaches to the "wings" of a proscenium theatre, those narrow passageways by which actors cross from their lives to their roles, and to the dark, radial aisles down which actors pass to the stage of an arena auditorium.

Having parted the curtain and crossed the "narrow bridge," the Noh actor arrives at a playing area which is no less than these a reminder of the hierophany he enacts. The Noh stage contains one piece of permanent scenery, a painted pine tree, and represents (sometimes by mere verbal convention, sometimes with the help of a simple prop) a holy place—most often, a tomb. Both pine tree and tomb mark the stage as a place of hierophanies.

Pound explained the pine tree as a "symbol of the unchanging";[52] and perhaps insofar as it is a *pine* tree, that is its meaning. But there is a more basic significance simply in the presence of a *tree* onstage. Virtually all mythologies make mention of an *axis mundi*, a great central pillar that leads, like the "narrow bridge," from our world to the next.[53] This pillar is imagined either as fashioned from a tree or, more often, simply *as* a tree. The Hindu Aśvattha, the Norse Yggdrasil, and the kabbalistic tree of life are all instances of this archetype.[54] Now as the shaman is the expert in negotiating the "narrow bridge," so he makes a specialty of climbing the cosmic tree.[55] The presence of a tree on the Noh stage is therefore an allusion to the shaman-actor's "climbing up and down" between the public and the script *illud tempus*.

F. A. C. Wilson points out that the tombs or shrines which comprise the usual settings for Noh plays are natural symbols of the intersection of human reality with some other kind of reality,[56] and as such, they bear a close affinity to sites of theatrical performance. In the West there is some evidence that tomb architecture may have influenced the evolution of the Renaissance stage;[57] and here, too, the connection is far from fortuitous. Mediaeval and Renaissance tomb sculpture customarily depict the moment of the buried person's awakening to new life.[58] Theatrical performance is also a moment in which life that has long been latent (that of the Image) suddenly comes back to life (that is, achieves presence in the body of the hungan-actor). As in other respects, so here: the Noh convention only makes the implicit, explicit. *All* theatre is an apparition at a tomb.

In the classical Greek theatre, even more clearly than in the Noh, the physical form of the stage is an ideogram for the kind of place a stage is.

The Greek stage (*Diagram 3*) was composed of two playing areas: the upstage *skene*, a long rectangular platform on which actors portraying individual characters from the *illud tempus* of tragic myth perform; and the downstage *orchestra*, a circular dancing-floor on which the chorus, portraying (as a rule) ordinary human society, perform.

The fact that the relation of *skene* to *orchestra* is that of a tangent to a circle is significant. A tangent can intersect a circle only momentarily, at a single point. As a rule, the *illud tempus* of a script and our human physical world do not intersect at all. But at the meeting-point of *skene* and *orchestra*, the eternal "plane" of the *illud tempus* (the *skene*) briefly intersects the daily "round" of our ordinary life (the *orches-*

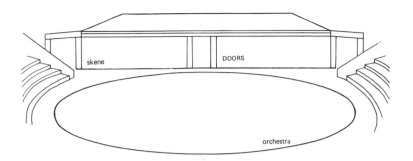

Diagram 3: The ancient Greek stage. *Drawing by Anne Geer.*

tra). This single moment of intersection occurs, of course, at the moment the Image achieves manifestation in the physical body of the actor—that is, at the moment of performance. Thus the very form of the Greek stage is a diagram of the structure of the theatrical event.

The doors just upstage of this point of intersection therefore assume the character of a "portal" through which the *illud tempus* passes into our world. I will say more about this symbolism in a moment, apropos of the proscenium arch.

The architecture of the Elizabethan public playhouse also suggests an attempt to have the place of hierophanies show, in its form, something of the process of hierophany. I have neither the knowledge nor the wish to become embroiled in the scholarly controversy surrounding the construction of these buildings.[59] The only aspects of their architecture that concern me are not, so far as I know, in serious dispute. These are: the central opening at the top of the playhouse; the pair of support pillars that ran from below the stage up toward this central opening; and the three-tiered construction of the performance space as a whole, comprising a vault-like understage, the stage floor itself, and an upper playing area surmounted by painted "heavens" and a rooftop machinery hut.

It has long been recognized that the structure of the Elizabethan public playhouse represented the cosmos. What

I wish to point out is how closely it represented a specifically *shamanic* cosmos (*Diagram 4*). For shamanism,

> There are three great cosmic regions, which can be succes-
> sively traversed because they are linked together by a central
> axis. This axis, of course, passes through an "opening," a
> "hole"; it is through this hole that the gods descend to earth
> and the dead to the subterranean regions; it is through the
> same hole that the soul of the shaman in ecstasy can fly up
> or down in the course of his celestial or infernal journeys.[60]

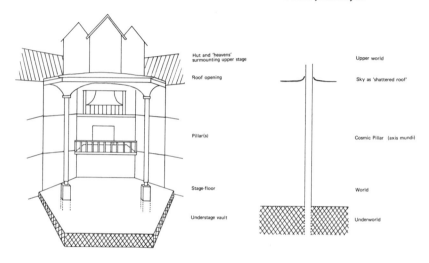

Diagram 4: Parallels between the Elizabethan public playhouse and the shamanic cosmos. *Drawing by Anne Geer.*

To each of the details of this world-picture corresponds an
architectural feature of the Elizabethan public playhouse.
The central opening at the top of the playhouse recalls the
roof-openings through which shamans are believed to set
out on their trips to the *illud tempus*[61]—a belief reflected in
the Buddhist expression "shattering the roof" as a metaphor
for ecstatic ascent.[62] The pillars reaching from below the
stage-floor up toward this opening suggest (as does the

painted pine of the Noh stage) the *axis mundi*, which the shaman climbs up or down to get to the *illud tempus*. And the three levels which these pillars connect—understage, stage-floor, and upper stage—correspond to the three levels which shamanism sees the *axis mundi* as connecting (and thereby enabling the shaman to traverse): underworld, earth, and sky.[63] The parallel becomes more striking when it is borne in mind that the "heaven"/hut above and the vault below not only make clear architectural equivalents to the upper and lower regions of the shamanic *illud tempus*, they also possess that property of an *illud tempus* which first led us to use the term in connection with theatre: the potentiality *for presence*. This hell and this heaven open upon our world. At any moment a god may descend from the hut, a demon start up through the trap. At any moment the noumena may *be there*.

What I am suggesting is that the Elizabethan public playhouse reflected in its structure not only the cosmos which is the site of human action (the stage which all the world is), but also that specifically theatrical cosmos, that space at once both intrapsychic and social, through which the shaman-actor pursues his journey from an audience to an Image.

In the post-Renaissance proscenium theatre, with curtain and darkened auditorium, the tendency for the architecture of the performance site to proclaim the hierophanic nature of performance reaches its peak.

As I have already suggested in connection with Noh, theatre curtains symbolize the veil which, in hierophany, is drawn aside from the *illud tempus*. When this revelatory curtain is set just behind a proscenium arch, the proscenium arch itself assumes the character of a threshold or portal: the veil/curtain drawn aside, we pass through the portal/arch into the *illud tempus* (or: the *illud tempus* passes outward under the portal/arch toward us).

Thresholds and portals are universally regarded as symbols of, or as actual sites of, hierophany:

> The threshold that separates the two spaces also indicates the distance between two modes of being, the profane and the religious. The threshold is the limit, the boundary, the frontier that distinguishes and opposes two worlds — and at the same time the paradoxical place where those worlds communicate, where passage from the profane to the sacred world becomes possible.[64]

Dream imagery, too, is full of doorways and portals—vaginal "gates of the dream," in Róheim's phrase,[65] through which, on falling asleep, one passes from this world (the waking state) into the uterine *illud tempus* of the unconscious.

Portal-like structures in the theatre are particularly susceptible to interpretation along these lines. I suggested earlier that the approach-ramp to the Noh stage, the wings of a Western theatre, and the upstage center doors of the ancient Greek *skene* can all best be understood as points of transit through which figures from the *illud tempus* enter our world. In the traditional Chinese theatre the entrances to the stage were actually *called* "doors of the shadows" or "doors of the souls,"[66] names which seem to reflect explicit awareness of this symbolism.

As for our present concern, the proscenium arch, there is historical evidence that it may in fact have evolved from such portal-like structures as the city gate[67] and the triumphal arch.[68] There is also, of course, considerable evidence that the proscenium arch came about as the result of attempts to adapt the picture frame to the task of framing a stage picture. (Certainly it has become customary to speak of the "picture-frame stage.") For our purposes it makes little difference which of these explanations is accepted. Picture frames are *themselves* portals or thresholds to the pictorial "other worlds" that can be glimpsed through them.

The darkening of the auditorium during performance, a custom which dates from the nineteenth century, is not at the present time peculiar to proscenium theatres, but was first practiced in them, and so is discussed in connection with them here. One may at first be inclined to view the significance of this practice in purely practical terms: a dark house focusses the attentiveness of an audience and increases the visibility of a stage. But even these practical considerations have a significance beyond the practical. Something that helps focus an audience's attentiveness on a manifestation deepens their capacity for receiving manifestations—and so is a sort of aid to meditation. Something that increases the visibility of a manifestation renders it more manifest—and so is itself part of the process of manifestation.

This way of understanding the darkened auditorium gains support from the role that darkness and darkening have traditionally played in the symbolism of religious and visionary experience. Many rituals—the Catholic Easter Vigil, for example—reflect the belief that total blackout is an indispensable preliminary for reestablishing the primordial perfection, the *illud tempus*, which is then made present by the kindling of innumerable flames.[69] On the level of visionary experience, too, one must walk in darkness to see a great light. Darkness is the traditional metaphor for the condition of a mind emptied of its usual concerns and ready to receive an intimation of the *illud tempus*.[70] Shamans often set off on their mystic journeys in darkness or near-darkness;[71] and clearly, since these are *dream* journeys into the unconscious (the "dark" side of the mind),[72] *night* is the appropriate time for them.

That the darkened auditorium is a "visionary dark" becomes still clearer if we examine our feelings at those moments when darkness engulfs the theatre completely: just before the start of a play, and during a scene change. The theatre's moments of darkness are far more than mere punctuation marks or rest-breaks. During a blackout one Image descends and another rises into our midst. Such spiritual transits are always accomplished in a moment of darkness:

the stroke of midnight, the hour of death, and so forth. If we let ourselves think about it, there is a level on which a blackout, like so much else having to do with the process of manifestation, makes us profoundly uneasy: anything in the world could be there when the lights come on—and whatever it is going to be is now heading toward us, through this darkness. We trust the actor to keep whatever he carries at a safe distance from us, and so the blackout is experienced more as a renewal of expectation than of uneasiness. But uneasiness is never altogether absent.

Freud attributes the fear of darkness in adults to "that infantile morbid anxiety from which the majority of human beings have never become quite free."[73] But as I suggested in the last chapter, when theatre encourages regressive behavior, it does so to make us aware of something about itself. Our anxiety during blackouts serves to remind us that this is a hierophany we are waiting on; that it will be a noumenon providing the light that comes up.

Such, then, is the meaning of the proscenium theatre, read as an architectural symbol. Through the portal between worlds (the proscenium), when the veil between worlds (the curtain) is lifted, the *illud tempus* issues forth to minds from which every extraneous concern has been extinguished (the darkened auditorium). Theatre construction can go no further in embodying the structure of the theatrical event.

I do not wish to sound as if I regard this as a triumph. At the outset of this chapter I raised the question of why so much twentieth-century theatre reform has begun with rejection of the proscenium stage. Copeau, Meyerhold, Artaud, Grotowski—figures who agree on little else, agree on this. Perhaps I can now attempt to answer that question. It is customary to explain rejection of the proscenium stage as stemming from a dislike of pictorialism as a scenic value or of voyeuristic passivity as an audience attitude. I would suggest that there is a more encompassing reason than either of these for attacking a style of theatre construction which turns the whole building into a model of the hierophanic process to be enacted there—namely, a sense that performance should be bringing home its *own* character as hierophany, that this should not have to be conveyed by the look of the performance *site*. Behind every outcry for a poor theatre and an empty space lies the desire to get manifestation out of the structure of the *place* and put it back where it belongs, in the structure of the *event*.

CHAPTER 5

Language

WHY should language be in the theatre? It is by no means an obvious question. An actor can often make an Image present solely by gesture (indeed, some Images *are* nothing more than patterns of gesture); and the scenic means account for whatever may be needed of the accompanying *illud tempus*.

A definition of language in the theatre as whatever happens to get said in the course of an action is not only uninformative, it rests on the assumption that language in the theatre just is what it is everywhere else. That would be surprising. Everything else that finds a place in the theatre—gesture, setting, light, and so on—finds its place by virtue of being able to manifest some aspect of the Image. Stage light does not just ensure visibility, it manifests otherness; stage blocking does not simply carry people across the room, it manifests relationship. There is nothing to be on the stage but a hierophany. If language has a place in theatre, it must have a share in the work of manifestation. The question: what does language do in the theatre? thus reduces to: what aspect of the Image does language manifest?

Clearly, its consciousness. Dramatic language renders the movements of consciousness *as verbal movement*. By "verbal movement" I do not mean exclusively, or even primarily, verbal rhythm. I use the term to include any variation in tone, syntax, imagery, or level of diction that can reflect a movement in consciousness. A speech in a play can be thought of as a kind of continuous moving graph, transcribing as aural-semantic patterns every slightest impulse and tremor in the consciousness "behind" it. I must emphasize that I am not offering this as a general theory of how language works, any more than I would put forward stage lighting as a general theory of optics. We are concerned only with the theatre. And if language is to figure in theatre, theatre must be able to make the same assumption about it that theatre makes about any of its resources: that that resource can become suffused with some aspect of the life of the Image; can become a hierophany. Language in the theatre is the hierophany of consciousness.

The "hierophanic" character of successful dramatic language becomes clear when one places a passage that lacks this quality side by side with another that possesses it. We can observe this contrast in the following pair of passages, the first from Ibsen's *Rosmersholm*, the second from Shakespeare's *Troilus and Cressida*. (Apropos of the Ibsen and other translated passages in this chapter: Even though my subject is nuances of language, I have felt free to use English-language versions in all instances, because what concerns us is the ability of a given passage to manifest consciousness in performance before an English-speaking audience, and this is not affected by whether the passage in its original language had more or less of the qualities I attribute to it in translation.)

ROSMER. This is the question I keep asking myself. Have we two been deceiving ourselves in calling our relationship a friendship?
REBECCA. You mean we ought to have called it——?
ROSMER. Love. Yes, Rebecca, I mean that. Even when Beata was alive, I thought only of you. You were the one I yearned for. With you I found a happiness that was calm and joyful and not based merely on sensuality. When you really think about it, Rebecca—we were like two children falling sweetly and sec-

retly in love. We made no demands, we dreamed no dreams. Wasn't that how you felt too? Tell me.

REBECCA. *(torn within herself)* Oh—I don't know what to reply to that.

ROSMER. And this life we lived so passionately—with each other and for each other—we mistook for friendship. No, Rebecca—our relationship has been a spiritual marriage—perhaps from the first moment we knew each other. So that I am guilty. I had no right to do this—no right, for Beata's sake.

REBECCA. No right to live in happiness? Do you believe that, John?

ROSMER. She saw our relationship through the eyes of *her* love. Condemned it by the measure of *her* love. She had to. Beata couldn't have judged us in any other way than she did.

[Ibsen, *Rosmersholm*, Act III][1]

In this excerpt the verbal surface, rather than manifesting consciousness, sheds doubt on it. The speakers' language is adequate to the subtlety of their thoughts ("so that . . . ," "by the measure of . . ."), but not to the anguish those thoughts are supposed to be causing them. It is difficult to believe that the emotions which the language claims are present could be present at so little cost to the language. Are "mistook" and "deceiving ourselves in calling" idioms in which people so deceived and mistaken acknowledge the fact? The capacity which Rosmer's diction shows him to possess for exactly comprehending his grief, belies it; that exactness has its origins in the perceptivity of Henrik Ibsen, not in the consciousness of John Rosmer. A stage direction is required to inform us that Rebecca is *"torn within herself"* because the language has not suffered a rent.

In the Shakespeare passage, on the other hand, the movement of the language exactly manifests the movements of the consciousness behind it:

CRESSIDA. Who's that?

(HELENUS passes.)

PANDARUS. That's Helenus. I marvel where Troilus is. That's Helenus. I think he went not forth today. That's Helenus.

CRESSIDA. Can Helenus fight, uncle?

PANDARUS. Helenus? no. Yes, he'll fight indifferent well.
I marvel where Troilus is. Hark! do you not hear the people
cry "Troilus"? Helenus is a priest.
    CRESSIDA. What sneaking fellow comes yonder?
                        (TROILUS passes.)
    PANDARUS. Where? Yonder? That's Deiphobus. 'Tis Troilus!
There's a man, niece! Hem! Brave Troilus! the prince of
chivalry!

                [Shakespeare, *Troilus and Cressida*, Act I, scene 2][2]

Pandarus has room in his thoughts for nothing but the immi-
nent arrival of Troilus; his niece's questions force him away
from this preoccupation, but his mind keeps zinging back to
it like a ball on a string. This circumstance of consciousness
determines every movement of his language. In his first speech
the phrase "That's Helenus" is thrice repeated because each
intervening recoil to the subject of Troilus has blotted out of
his mind any recollection of having already answered a question on another subject. The reply he makes to Cressida's
next question, as to whether Helenus can fight ("Helenus? no.
Yes . . .") again shows his difficulty in fixing his mind on any
subject other than Troilus. His "no" means "not in comparison
with Troilus!"; his "yes" is a grudging concession—not so
much to Helenus's abilities themselves, as to the necessity of
considering a Matter Not Troilus on its own merits. The belated position of "Helenus is a priest" reflects a belated impulse to give subjects other than Troilus their due. And
finally, we note the absence of the self-correcting "no" which
we would expect between "That's Deiphobus" and "'Tis
Troilus!" Pandarus feels no need to retract his earlier misidentification because, in the excitement of seeing Troilus,
all recollection of having *made* an earlier misidentification
flies out of his head.

    Now let us juxtapose two *verse* passages that reflect the
contrast between language that does not move with consciousness and language that does. The first is from Congreve's
The Mourning Bride; the second, from *Macbeth*.

OSMYN. O impotence of Sight! Mechanick Sense,
Which to exterior Objects ow'st thy Faculty,
Not seeing of Election, but Necessity.
Thus do our Eyes, as do all common Mirrours,
Successively reflect succeeding Images;
Not what they would, but must; a star, or Toad:
Just as the Hand of Chance administers.
     [Congreve, *The Mourning Bride*, Act II, scene 2] [3]

Considered as a passage of meditative poetry, this cannot be dismissed as unskillful or uninteresting writing. It has a suggestive precision of diction ("election," "administers"); it is elegantly cadenced as a blank verse paragraph; it makes unobtrusive use of sound to reinforce sense (the aural disparity between "toad" and "star" emphasizes their disparity as objects; the echo of "successively" in "succeeding" brings home the mechanical nature of the process). But it is not meditative poetry; it is meant as the dramatic utterance of a man in a desperate situation (Osmyn's realization of the "impotence of Sight" is brought on by his just having had to watch helplessly as the woman he loves withdraws from him, perhaps forever). As such, it is not only inadequate but a victim of its own verbal adequacy. Its poetic success is due to the fact that it possesses, as verse, the very quality which, as dramatic utterance, it is supposed to be expressing the want of: conscious control. One simply cannot believe that these assured cadences are issuing from feelings of "impotence." As in the *Rosmersholm* excerpt, expression, rather than manifesting consciousness, gives it the lie.

By contrast, the following well-known lines from *Macbeth* are an exact verbal hierophany of the event in consciousness that underlies them:

MACBETH. Will all great Neptune's ocean wash this blood
Clean from my hand? No, this my hand will rather
The multitudinous seas incarnadine
Making the green one red.
     [Shakespeare, *Macbeth*, Act II, scene 2] [4]

The sudden rise in the level of diction at "multitudinous seas incarnadine" reflects the sudden opening out of Macbeth's field of vision as he imagines his personal guilt expanding to stain all nature. The return to simple diction in the next line conveys Macbeth's wonder at the sudden, awful uniformity which his act of self-projection has brought upon things: a whole world the color of a guilt!

I have made a point of going through the same process of comparison for prose and for verse so as to emphasize that neither is intrinsically more hierophanic than the other. Each has its characteristic resources for manifesting consciousness; and each, as we have seen, can succeed or fail in employing those resources. The basic distinction in dramatic language is not between prose and verse, but between language that *moves with consciousness* and language that takes its movement from something else—an ambition on the part of the playwright to write "good prose" or "rich verse," to convey (as in the Ibsen passage) psychological nuance or (as in the Congreve) interesting reflections.

"Does it move with consciousness?" may seem a modest enough criterion. The radical consequences come of taking it as the only one. The prose/verse distinction is only one of the familiar ways of classifying and evaluating dramatic language for which it leaves no place. Fidelity to "speech rhythms," for example, can no longer be regarded as inevitably to the good: Are there not movements of consciousness that do not keep to the channels of colloquial speech? As for elaborateness (whether of syntax, diction, image, or all three), it can neither be automatically approved as eloquent, nor automatically deplored as inflated; again, everything depends on whose consciousness the elaborate language is supposed to be emerging from—and (as the *Macbeth* excerpt shows) at what moment. And most emphatically, historical period and social class count for nothing in determining how a theatre character may speak. *As awareness grows brighter, language grows more capable*: that is the one inviolable canon of dramatic speech. The only limit on a character's ability to manifest consciousness in language is whatever limit there may be on his consciousness itself.

If the only legitimate role for language in the theatre is as the hierophany of consciousness, why is this a role that language in contemporary theatre is so seldom seen to play? Indeed, why does language play so slight a role of *any* kind in the work of so many contemporary playwrights? The reasons for this take us beyond the function of language in the theatrical event—take us, in fact, beyond theatre altogether—and we shall consider them in due course. First, however, I should like to look at the work of some contemporary playwrights who *have* tried to give language its share in the work of theatrical expression. This will involve examining a wide variety of experiments, but we shall find that our criterion holds, down the line. Where a modern playwright is successful with language, it is because he has found a way of making it move with consciousness; where another has failed, it has been as a result of his trying to make it do, or be, something else.

We shall look first at three passages of successful dramatic writing by Yeats, Beckett, and Pinter, respectively. Different as the passages are, each will be seen to have the movement of the consciousness that speaks it. Then we shall examine three passages which illustrate the appealing but ultimately invalid attempts of Synge, O'Casey, and Eliot to "steal" vitality for dramatic language by harnessing that language to some movement other than that of the speaker's consciousness. Finally, we shall look at examples of the two most extreme experiments with language in twentieth-century theatre: the Expressionist "telegraph style" and the Futurist *parole in libertà*. These experiments show how, even when language is presented in such a way as to stress its inadequacies, adherence to the basic "with consciousness" principle of dramatic speech becomes the means of making the critique.

The opening speeches of Yeats's *Purgatory* are windows
to their speakers' consciousness:

> BOY. Half-door, hall door,
> Hither and thither day and night,
> Hill or hollow, shouldering this pack,
> Hearing you talk.
> OLD MAN.   Study that house.
> I think about its jokes and stories;
> I try to remember what the butler
> Said to a drunken gamekeeper
> In mid-October, but I cannot.
> If I cannot, none living can.
> Where are the jokes and stories of a house,
> Its threshold gone to patch a pig-sty?
> [Yeats, *Purgatory*][5]

In the Boy's speech the rhythm of a weary journey on foot
has established itself as the very movement of consciousness,
giving each heavily caesuraed line the quality of a left-and-
a-right trudge. This interiorized movement of consciousness
is so pervasive as to force any particular thought that may
arise to occur within its rhythm—even when, as in line 3, two
elements not really in binary relation ("hill or hollow" and
"shouldering this pack") get forced into the slog-slog rhythm
anyway. Also reflective of the Boy's consciousness is the
pairing: "Half-door, hall door"—the residuum, condensed
down to a single pair of details floating in the mind, of innumerable knockings and receptions.

The lines of the Old Man, too, manifest the tendency
of consciousness as verbal tendency. His speech is a strange
blend of unmistakably personal recollections ("butler,"
"gamekeeper," "mid-October," a "threshold gone to patch a
pig-sty") delivered as unmistakably public pronouncements
("I think," "I try," "I cannot"). Throughout the play the Old
Man attempts to affirm a continuity between his personal
life and the life of the great house whose ruins he stands before. The appropriation of a tone that claims for inner mental

processes the status of public events is the clear verbal equivalent of this attempt.

The following, fairly typical excerpt from *Waiting for Godot* shows Samuel Beckett's great skill in making language hierophanic:

> ESTRAGON. (*coldly*) There are times when I wonder if it wouldn't be better for us to part.
> VLADIMIR. You wouldn't go far.
> ESTRAGON. That would be too bad, really too bad. (*Pause*) Wouldn't it, Didi, be really too bad? (*Pause*) When you think of the beauty of the way. (*Pause*) And the goodness of the wayfarers. (*Pause. Wheedling.*) Wouldn't it, Didi?
> VLADIMIR. Calm yourself.
> ESTRAGON. (*voluptuously*) Calm . . . Calm . . . The English say cawm. (*Pause*) You know the story of the Englishman in the brothel?
> [Beckett, *Waiting for Godot*, Act I][6]

The additive rhythm of Estragon's second speech—"too bad" becomes "really too bad" becomes "Wouldn't it . . . be really too bad"—exactly manifests Estragon's increasingly insistent demand for response; it is the verbal equivalent of a succession of sharper and sharper pokes in the ribs. And as Estragon becomes distracted from this aim, his language clearly graphs the lessening urgency: "calm" softens into English "cawm" softens into a joke about an Englishman.

The recurring phrases in the following excerpt from Pinter's *The Caretaker* recall the recurrent "That's Helenus" in the speech of Shakespeare's Pandarus quoted earlier:

> DAVIES. You mean you're throwing me out? You can't do that. Listen man, listen man, I don't mind, you see, I don't mind, I'll stay, I don't mind, I'll tell you what, if you don't want to change beds, we'll keep it as it is, I'll stay in the same bed, maybe if I can get a stronger piece of sacking, like, to go over the window, keep out the draught, that'll do it, what do you say, we'll keep it as it is?
> [Pinter, *The Caretaker*, Act III][7]

Here, too, recurrence of phrase betrays a nagging preoccupation. But the fact that it is *three* phrases that are repeated, and that they are all expressions of conciliation, reflects the peculiar mental strain Davies is under. The person to whom he is speaking must not be allowed to stop paying attention (whence the repeated "Listen man"), nor must he be made to feel that he is being opposed (whence the repeated "I don't mind"), nor must he receive the impression that something is being asked of him (whence the repeated "we'll keep it as it is"), for any one of these possibilities would constitute an excuse for terminating the situation, an "out." Davies's dashing about from phrase to phrase is a desperate attempt to keep all these exits covered at once.

Synge, O'Casey, and T. S. Eliot all tried to make the enormous vitality of common speech serve as a source of vitality for dramatic writing. The results, in all cases, are attractive failures. For the rhythms of common speech are alive insofar as they manifest *what a society has been through,* as distinguished from *what a consciousness is going through.*

Here are the words of Maurya, Synge's *mater dolorosa* in *Riders to the Sea*, upon learning of the death of her one remaining son:

> MAURYA. They are all gone now, and there isn't anything more the sea can do to me. . . . I'll have no call now to be up crying and praying when the wind breaks from the south, and you can hear the surf is in the east, and the surf is in the west, making a great stir with the two noises, and they hitting one on the other. . . . They're all together this time, and the end is come. May the almighty God have mercy on Bartley's soul, and on Michael's soul, and on the souls of Sheamus and Patch, and Stephen and Shawn; and may He have mercy on my soul, Nora, and on the soul of every one is left living in the world.
> [Synge, *Riders to the Sea*][8]

Rather than the verbal rhythms here coming from *within her,* it seems as if she is locating herself *within them*—and thereby locating herself within the rhythms of life as experienced in her world, of which they seem the reflection. The syntactic patterns, even the word choices, seem formulaic, *there to assent to*; and Maurya's acquiescence in them reveals that she, like the Old Man in *Purgatory*, seeks to be caught up in a life larger than her own, to move—literally—in the world's rhythms. But in contrast with the Old Man's speech in the Yeats excerpt, individual consciousness here cannot be heard pushing out from behind the public idiom.

By contrast, the following speech of O'Casey's seems, at first glance, charmingly individuated:

> MRS. GOGAN. Y'oul'rip of a blasted liar, me weddin' ring's been well earned be twenty years be th'side o' me husband, now takin' his rest in heaven, married to me be Father Dempsey, in th' Chapel o' Saint Jude's, in th' Christmas Week of eighteen hundhred an' ninety-five; an' any kid, livin' or dead, that Jinnie Gogan's had since, was got between the bordhers of th' Ten Commandments! An' that's more than some o' you can say that are kep' from th' dhread o' desthruction be a few drowsy virtues, that th' first whisper of temptation lulls into a sleep, that'll know one sin from another only on th'day of their last anointin', an' that use th' innocent light o' th' shinin' stars to dip into th' sins of a night's diversion.
>
> [O'Casey, *The Plough and the Stars*, Act II][9]

Yet all O'Casey's people talk more or less like this—anu not because they are insufficiently differentiated on the level of "character." What gives Mrs. Gogan's language its vitality is a series of suggestive confusions, none of them particularly Mrs. Gogan's. The expression "between the bordhers of th' Ten Commandments," for example, is the product of one of those collisions of distinct idioms that often occur in the mind of a half-educated person. To the hearer, such a confusion may sound subtle, even witty; but there is nothing going on in Mrs. Gogan's mind that corresponds to that impression. The "rise" in the language is there only for the audience; it is

not the result of any rise in awareness in the speaker. If the
language here manifests anything, it manifests Mrs. Gogan's
membership in a class that is subject to certain linguistic
confusions—for example, running together the diction of
nursery poems ("th' innocent light o' th' shinin' stars") and
melodrama subtitles ("a night's diversion"). But that class
membership is not what is going on at this moment in the
consciousness of Mrs. Gogan.

Eliot, at least in the first of the two passages quoted
below, is more successful at making tendencies of class usage
manifest movements of individual consciousness:

> CELIA.   An awareness of solitude.
> But that sounds so flat. I don't mean simply
> That there's been a crash: though indeed there has been.
> It isn't simply the end of an illusion
> In the ordinary way, or being ditched.
> Of course that's something that's always happening
> To all sorts of people, and they get over it
> More or less, or at least they carry on.
> No. I mean that what has happened has made me aware
> That I've always been alone. That one always is alone.
> Not simply the ending of one relationship,
> Not even simply finding that it never existed—
> But a revelation about my relationship
> With *everybody*. Do you know—
> It no longer seems worth while to speak to anyone!
>   [Eliot, *The Cocktail Party*, Act II][10]

> CELIA.   I cannot argue.
> It's not that I'm afraid of being hurt again.
> Nothing again can either hurt or heal.
> I have thought at moments that the ecstasy is real
> Although those who experience it may have no reality.
> For what happened is remembered like a dream
> In which one is exalted by intensity of loving
> In the spirit, a vibration of delight
> Without desire, for desire is fulfilled
> In the delight of loving.
>   [Eliot, *The Cocktail Party*, later in Act II][11]

"Crash," "being ditched," "carry on," and "get over it" are the pallid slang natural to a girl of Celia's class; but *her* use of these phrases here manifests a struggle that is peculiarly hers: the effort to comprehend a dawning religious vocation within accustomed categories of expression and feeling. In her use of "revelation," for example, the literal, Christian meaning of the word struggles for primacy with a society-lady's way of using it ("it was simply a *revelation* to me"); and this struggle between the society-lady and the Christian is, of course, precisely Celia's own.

In the second speech, however, the tension becomes too much for the language to handle. From the gratuitous alliteration "hurt or heal" on, the language ceases to be heard as issuing from an individual consciousness. The "I" of line 4 is not Celia any more, but some generalized meditative third-person; the tense of "have thought" is not a time in Celia's past but a stage along the *via contemplativa*. In the final five lines the speaking voice has become that of the *Four Quartets*.

Expressionist "telegraph style" and Futurist *parole in libertà* were meant as challenges to the principle that dramatic speech reflects movements of consciousness. However, specific examples of these styles show a surprising tendency to confirm this principle.

The Expressionists sought to reduce the status of language in the theatre by showing that any speech could be expressed by a "telegram" of its content. For example:

> (*Opera. First-tier box. The box curtains are drawn. The box at the right is unoccupied.* ALEXANDER, THE YOUTH, THE GIRL *are seated.*)
> USHERETTE. Opera glasses?
> NEWSBOY. Extra—Sensational burglary.
> THE YOUTH. I am no more.
> VOICE. (*from below*) Intermission!
> ALEXANDER. We lie in the grave
> THE GIRL. (*pressing her hands to her abdomen*)
> The child is stirring
> VOICE. (*from below*) A chair!
> THE YOUTH. Eternity

ALEXANDER. The gates are open
VOICE. The finale begins!
THE YOUTH. I see the world. . . .
TENOR SOLO. "Donna è mobile."
    [Hasenclever, *Humanity*, Act II, scene 5][12]

It will be noted that practically every "speech" in the excerpt has roughly the same two-accent stress pattern: "Ínter-
míssion," "We líe in the gráve," "Dónna è móbile," etc.
If one verbal rhythm will do to express everything in our
experience from a hawker's cry ("Ópera glásses") to a
moment of vision ("I sée the wórld"), that is a terrible indictment of our experience. But it is *not* an indictment of
our language. We are vulnerable to criticism for leading
lives to which a language so straitened is adequate; but such
as the lives are, the language *is* adequate to it. It is consciousness itself that has suffered trivialization; language
continues the faithful mirror of consciousness.

Remo Chiti's Futurist playlet *Words* depicts an angry
crowd milling around a gate. The entire dialogue is made up
of the overheard fragments of remarks that occasionally
succeed in detaching themselves from the general murmur:

    . . . and why ARE THEY also a . . .
    . . . exactly! And in FIFTY YEARS no . . .
    . . . go there! THAT IS enough . . .
    . . . of him who WAITS some more . . .
    . . . that is SOMETHING that doesn't work . . .
    . . . he put it BY THE DOOR and he said . . .
    . . . it is better FROM him . . .
    . . . he has a PALACE for . . .
    . . . and you don't UNDERSTAND that it isn't . . .
    . . . prove he DOESN'T wish to say . . .
    . . . and it doesn't INTEREST YOU AT ALL that . . .
    . . . yesterday . . . TODAY . . . tomorrow . . .
    . . . and FINALLY he said . . .
            [Chiti, *Words*][13]

Here again, as in the Expressionist scene, the speeches all
have the same stress pattern: in this case, ◡ ′ ◡. But the

implication of the uniformity here is quite different. Chiti is making the point that language cannot be relied on to *continuously* manifest the movement of consciousness: in any given speech there may well be only *one* moment when the movement of feeling gets the verbal surface under its control. However, *that is the moment in each speech that Chiti elects to show*: the bit of language in which each member of the crowd is, for a moment, able to make his rhythm of plaintive insistence perceptible as a plaintively insistent verbal rhythm (ᴜ ᛧ ᴜ). In other words, Chiti's aim may be to point out the undependability of the "as consciousness, so speech" criterion; but insofar as he includes only those moments when that criterion is observed, he observes it.

The preceding examples convey the impression that whenever dramatic language fails, it is as the result of individual playwrights' failures to understand how language functions in the theatre. Yet when one considers how pervasive in our theatre is a certain discomfort with language— a discomfort not limited to playwrights but shared by actors, directors and audiences alike—it is difficult to believe that nothing more is involved than a large number of individual misunderstandings.

We have heard many explanations of why language has atrophied in the modern theatre. There is the still prevalent naturalist aesthetic to discourage a writer from "trying anything" with language; and there is the achievement of the great verse dramatists to intimidate anyone who tries. There is the renascence of the view that theatre is primarily a scenic or gestural art, and the corresponding inclination to dismiss as "undramatic" plays that are "all talk" or even "talky." And perhaps underlying all the rest is a suspicion that language itself—sullied by political manipulation, surpassed in exactness by mathematics and in suggestiveness by graphic imagery—has become too blurred and compromised an instrument for our needs.

While all of these may be contributing factors, none of them can be the root cause. Dramatic language is the manifestation of consciousness. The only way it can decline is when it is no longer trusted to manifest consciousness. Modern theatre is afflicted by precisely this mistrust—to the degree that one of our leading playwrights, Pinter, can tell a group of young drama students: "The speech we hear is an indication of that we don't hear. It is a necessary avoidance, a violent, sly, anguished or mocking smoke screen which keeps the other in its place. . . . One way of looking at speech is to say it is a constant strategem to cover nakedness."[14] In the work of Pinter himself, language continues to be manifestational: the very effort of consciousness to *stay hidden* is often what it manifests. However, many theatre practitioners share Pinter's mistrust without sharing his ability to capitalize on it; and for them language has virtually ceased to figure among the resources of dramatic expression.

One of the most characteristic symptoms of this tendency in contemporary theatre practice is the fascination with "subtexts." The term is Stanislavski's, and is defined by him as

> the manifest, the inwardly felt expression of a human being in a part, which flows uninterruptedly beneath the words of the text, giving them life and a basis for existing. The subtext is a web of innumerable, varied inner patterns inside a play and a part, woven from "magic ifs," given circumstances, all sorts of figments of the imagination, inner movements, objects of attention, smaller and greater truths and a belief in them, adaptations, adjustments and other similar elements. It is the subtext that makes us say the words we do in a play.[15]

It is ironic that the belief in subtexts should work against the expressive potential of language, since it was precisely in the hopes of getting actors and directors to *see more* in language that Stanislavski introduced subtextual analysis. Words, he insisted, must be regarded as "sent up" by consciousness, not just as spoken. Is not this the very view of language for which I have been arguing?

There is one all-important difference. Dramatic language does not simply have the movement of consciousness *behind* it; it must *itself have* that movement as its own. Practitioners of subtextual analysis, however, tend to assume, with Pinter, that the actual words of the text, far from manifesting subtextual feeling, represent a more or less willful attempt to conceal it. The discrepancy between consciousness and expression which, in the Congreve and Ibsen passages I analyzed, comes across as a flaw, is thus accepted as the norm. The words of the text are thought of as an opacity through which the actor, by one means or another, must cause subtextual light to shine:

> A former actor of Stanislavski's Moscow Theatre . . . at his audition . . . was asked by the famous director to make forty different messages from the phrase *Segodnja večerom*, "This evening," by diversifying its expressive tint. He made a list of some forty emotional situations, then emitted the given phrase in accordance with each of these situations, which his audience had to recognize only from the changes in the sound shape of the same two words. . . . Most of the messages were correctly and circumstantially decoded by Muscovite listeners.[16]

This is, if true, a mark of great skill on the part of the actor—but what function does it leave for the two words in question? If the actor can manifest almost anything *through* them, what do *they* manifest?

It would, however, be getting things backward to identify a belief in subtexts as the *cause* of the decline of language in the theatre. Rather, it has been a widespread mistrust of language as the vehicle of consciousness—a mistrust which extends far beyond the boundaries of theatre—that has created an atmosphere favorable to a preoccupation with subtexts.

Attacks on the belief that language reflects movements of consciousness have come, in our time, from philosophy, from linguistics and psycholinguistics, from psychology and psychoanalysis, and, most recently, from semiotics. I have no competence—and, really, no reason—to try to "refute" the contentions of experts in all these fields. It is not a question of theatre holding one "theory" and each of these disciplines another. The view that language reflects movements of consciousness is not a theory advocated by theatre, but an expressive convention of theatre. What interests us is to see how recent discoveries in each of these fields are making it an increasingly difficult convention to work within.

Ludwig Wittgenstein, perhaps the most influential philosopher of this century, evolved in the course of his career two theories of language so different that the second may almost be said to constitute a recantation of the first. Greatly as these theories differ, on one crucial point they are in accord: early or late, Wittgenstein was profoundly skeptical of the view that language manifests consciousness. In the earlier period this skepticism took the form of doubts about language: "Language disguises the thought; so that from the external form of the clothes one cannot infer the form of the thought they clothe, because the external form of the clothes is constructed with quite another object than to let the form of the body be recognized."[17] The metaphor of expression as the "dress" of thought has been used since the Renaissance to impugn the reliability of language; for what is "dress" may be only "fancy dress," that is (as here), misleading disguise. In the later writings the doubt falls upon consciousness itself: "I have been trying in all this to remove the temptation to think that there '*must* be' what is called a mental process of thinking, hoping, wishing, believing, etc., independent of the process of expressing a thought, a hope, a wish, etc."[18] A sentence, Wittgenstein argues, should be regarded as a direct picture or "projection" of the situation it corresponds to (in the sense that a flat map is the projection of a globe): there is no need to posit some shadowy middle term called a "mental process." Clearly, if this is so, there is no question of language reflecting consciousness, because there is no consciousness to reflect. (Neither, of course, would it be justifiable to regard language as a veil drawn over a subtext; for there is nothing over which to draw the veil.)

Most linguists would not go so far as to deny that some sort of mental process occurs when a sentence is spoken. However, the relations that linguists have discovered between sentence and process do not encourage a hope that the movement of the former can be relied upon to reflect the movement of the latter. Chomsky, for example, argues for the presence in every sentence of a *deep structure* and a *surface structure*, and affirms a definite connection between them:

> We can . . . distinguish the *surface structure* of the sentence, the organization into categories and phrases that is directly associated with the physical signal, from the underlying *deep structure*, also a system of categories and phrases, but with a more abstract character. Thus the surface structure of the sentence "A wise man is honest" might analyze it into the subject "a wise man" and the predicate "is honest." The deep structure, however, will be rather different. It will, in particular, extract from the complex idea that constitutes the subject of the surface structure an underlying proposition with the subject "man" and the predicate "be wise." In fact, the deep structure . . . is a system of two propositions, neither of which is asserted, but which interrelate in such a way as to express the meaning of the sentence "A wise man is honest."[19]

The experiments of psycholinguists tend, on the whole, to confirm Chomsky's model:

> In one experiment . . . subjects were required to remember lists of two types of passive sentences:
> (1) Gloves were made by tailors.
> (2) Gloves were made by hand.
> These two sentences have the same surface structure, but different deep structures. Underlying (1) is an assertion that

tailors make gloves; underlying (2) is an assertion that some-body makes gloves, and that this process is done by hand.

Blumenthal aided subjects in recalling sentences by giving them the final noun ("tailors" or "hand") as a prompt. He found that nouns corresponding to the underlying sub-ject ("tailors") were much more successful memory aids than nouns like "hand," which are not part of the basic underlying structure. . . . The difference in recall must be attributed to the differing functions which the prompt words perform in the underlying structures of these sentences, since they seem to have no significant difference in terms of their surface position. These experiments make it quite clear that sentence processing must take place on two levels, as described in current linguistic theory.[20]

Now the fact that deep structure and surface structure are thus clearly related would seem to justify rather than undermine confidence in a manifestational view of language. But the rules of transformation, which, in practice, govern the relation, allow for endless shifts and exceptions. On the one hand, a single deep structure may produce sentences wholly different in tone and implication: for example, "She is a girl I love" and "She's a girl, I love her" might conceivably both proceed from the same deep structure. Conversely, sen-tences quite similar in verbal movement may be the product of wholly different deep structures, as in the example just quoted: "Gloves were made by tailors" and "Gloves were made by hand." "It is clear, in short," Chomsky writes, "that the surface structure is often misleading and uninformative."[21]

The French semiotic critics have attempted to extend Chomsky's categories of "deep" and "surface" structure from the analysis of single sentences to the analysis of longer ver-bal units: poems, stories, speeches from plays. This extension of the concept in the direction of theatre only makes clearer the challenge which it presents to a manifestational view of language. The semiotician is ready enough to grant that there exists "a certain isomorphism between expression as a whole and content as a whole." But, he hastens to add, "it must not be expected that this correspondence will be appar-

ent from the words in their linear sequence."[22] This means
that the words of, say, a dramatic speech must be taken out
of their order in the text and rearranged according to some
atemporal principle (as embodied in a pair of axes, a rule of
transformation, a chart, etc.) before their relation to the deep
structure that produced them can become visible. However,
it is only in their temporal sequence that words move with
consciousness; so whatever is manifested by rearranging them
in some other fashion, it is not a movement of consciousness.

Of course strictly speaking, neither Chomsky nor the
semioticians are really concerned with the reflection in
speech of a mentalistic "consciousness"; for them, both
"deep" and "surface" structure refer to levels within the language process itself. If we put the question in specifically
psychological terms—that is, as one concerning the relation
between verbal behavior and brain activity—the difficulty of
making a case for language as manifestation becomes still
greater. First of all, there is the physiological fact that, "since
central motor programming in the nervous system is much
more rapid than peripheral execution, there is always a tendency to anticipate features of subsequent phonemes and
persist in features of antecedent phonemes",[23] that is, language and thought move at different rates. But far more disturbing is the suggestion of the great Russian psychologist
Vygotsky that consciousness is, by its very origins, doomed
to uncommunicativeness. According to Piaget, the speech of
the young child is "egocentric"; that is, the child

> does not bother to know to whom he is speaking nor whether
> he is being listened to. He talks either for himself or for the
> pleasure of associating anyone who happens to be there with
> the activity of the moment. This talk is egocentric . . . chiefly
> because he does not attempt to place himself at the point
> of view of his hearer. The child asks for no more than ap-
> parent interest, though he has the illusion . . . of being heard
> and understood.[24]

In the view of Piaget himself, egocentric speech gradually
vanishes as the child undergoes socialization. But Vygotsky

suggested another fate for it. According to him, egocentric speech does not go away, it goes within;[25] that is, it is gradually internalized to become the silent thought of adult consciousness: "In the process, egocentric speech becomes more and more abbreviated and idiosyncratic, eventually becoming inner speech, or verbal thought, qualitatively different from outer speech."[26] If Vygotsky is right, the death-blow has been struck to theatre's convention of language as the manifestation of consciousness. How can consciousness be manifested by language when consciousness is itself the survival of a premanifestational stage of language, and thus "qualitatively different from outer speech"?

This "qualitative difference" is sharpened into something like enmity in Freud's theory of slips of the tongue, as set forth in *The Psychopathology of Everyday Life*. "There . . . runs through my thoughts," wrote Freud, "a continuous current of 'personal reference', of which I generally have no inkling, but which betrays itself by" so-called Freudian slips.[27] As was the case with Chomsky's deep and surface structures, it might seem at first that this is evidence in favor of the view of language as manifestation. Is not the implication that nothing ever happens in speech except as the result of an event in consciousness? But also implicit in Freud's view is the assumption that language and consciousness are inevitably at odds with one another. Language is envisioned as a sort of sentinel which consciousness—or rather, *un*consciousness—must elude in order to find its way into articulation. "The true thoughts," as Stekel wrote of a proof-reading error, "broke through the emotional statement with elemental force."[28] Consciousness manifests itself through language only in despite of language; verbal structure does not so much reflect consciousness as suffer deformation by it. It is difficult to think of a position further removed from confidence in language-as-manifestation than this view of the spoken word as a blown cover.

Returning to the theatre in search of evidence for the effect of such views, we shall not find that Freudian slips, egocentric speech, and misconnected deep structures have become the norm of dramatic writing: the influence has been subtler than that. Nevertheless, we recognize a play like *The Bald Soprano*, in which practically every line *is* a Freudian slip (e. g., "Take a circle, caress it, and it will turn vicious") as presenting us with the truth of our language experience. It is customary to say that *The Bald Soprano* dramatizes "the failure to communicate"; but in fact the characters seem able to communicate perfectly well:

> MR. SMITH. Oh, my dear, this is not so serious. The Fire Chief is an old friend of the family. His mother courted me, and I knew his father. He asked me to give him my daughter in marriage if ever I had one. And he died waiting.
> MR. MARTIN. That's neither his fault, nor yours.
> [Ionesco, *The Bald Soprano*][29]

The *sub*texts of such speeches are rational and approximately comprehensible both to the other characters and to us. But something happens to these rational subtexts "on the way up" into language: somewhere the wires get crossed, with the result that an intelligible movement of consciousness comes to be expressed by all the wrong words. The channels of interpersonal communication are still functioning; it is the channel from consciousness to expression *within each speaker* that has broken down: in other words, the process of manifestation itself.

The Austrian playwright Peter Handke has made a whole play out of the struggle of a single word upward from consciousness to expression. His *Calling for Help* consists entirely of a series of paragraphs like the following, to be read aloud by several speakers:

> the queen was wearing a new hat: NO. unknown is accused of having tipped over several gravestones: NO. the actor suffered a swooning attack while onstage: NO. a moist lip was the cause for the murder: NO. the bones were laid to their final rest in complete silence: NO. workers at that time

were living in inhuman conditions: NO. two nations are entering into a nonagression pact: NO. the newspaper did not
appear yesterday: NO. the moon moved between sun and
earth precisely according to calculation: NO. the ruler went
on foot: NO.

[Handke, *Calling for Help*][30]

"The speakers' objective," says Handke, "is to show the way
to the sought-after word HELP." The play is therefore over at
the moment when "a single speaker instantly speaks the word
HELP by himself, neither expressing gladness with it nor that
he is seeking help. The word HELP is uttered that way once"
(Handke, *Calling for Help*).[31] Clearly, it is not actual help
that is being sought, but the word that corresponds to the impulse in consciousness to cry for help; all the rest of the lines
are just so many wrong turnings "on the way to the word." If
in Ionesco the difficulty of crossing the treacherous void between mind and tongue has left its mark on virtually every
line of dialogue, in Handke that difficult crossing has become
the action of the play itself.

There is a Dada play by Tristan Tzara called *The Gas
Heart*, in which six characters named Eye, Ear, Mouth, Nose,
Neck, and Eyebrow mutter nonsense while "the gas heart
walks slowly around, circulating widely."[32] One can hardly
imagine a better metaphor for consciousness fitfully in
touch, or continually dropping out of touch, with its means
of exteriorization. R. D. Laing quotes a patient for whom
Tzara's bizarre metaphor was a psychic reality: "My real
self is away down—it used to be just at my throat, but now
it's gone further down. I'm losing myself. It's getting deeper
and deeper. I'm behind the bridge of my nose—I mean, my
consciousness is there."[33] That patient was a schizophrenic.
And "schizophrenic" must be the verdict on a theatre in
which an unbridgeable (or unreliably bridged) gap between
subtext and text, between consciousness and expression, has
established itself as the norm.

Certainly schizophrenia is more than a speech disorder.
But inability or unwillingness to verbalize accurately is one

of its earliest symptoms—indeed, sometimes suffices for a diagnosis of the disease.[34] And it is these very schizophrenic speech symptoms which have become the accepted conventions of language use in our theatre. The schizophrenic girl who repeated over and over again nonsense syllables of which "only the sound, the rhythm of the pronunciation had sense [and] through them I lamented "[35] would have passed with flying colors the Moscow Art Theatre audition described earlier, where the candidate was required to repeat one phrase so many times that it *became* nonsense, but capable (as for the disturbed girl) of conveying all subtexts. And no one would have had to explain *Calling for Help* to the schizophrenic patient who declared: "Being crazy is like one of those nightmares where you try to call for help and no sound comes out."[36] The following two sentences might be speeches from *The Bald Soprano*:

> A boy threw a stone at me to make an understanding between myself and the purpose of wrongdoing.

> I was transferred due to work over here due to methodical change of environment.[37]

In fact, they are the utterances of schizophrenics. Of course, not every contemporary play is as frank about its language problem as *The Bald Soprano*. But the impression which the verbal movement of so many contemporary plays gives of being impervious to modification by any pressure of mind or feeling "from behind" proceeds from the same refusal to trust language with a movement of consciousness that afflicts the schizophrenic.

While I cannot claim to be using the term with full clinical precision, I do mean something more, when I describe attitudes toward language in our theatre as "schizophrenic," than just that they are in some sense "unhealthy." What distinguishes schizophrenia from other mental diseases is that it affects not so much consciousness itself as the ability to *manifest* consciousness:

Even when the schizophrenic is in a state of physical and mental collapse suggesting dementia, he nonetheless remains in possession of his mental life and intelligence, often experiencing vivid sensations which he is unable to exteriorize.[38]

The schizophrenic mind, as both Freud and Jung emphasized,[39] is likely to be working far more coherently than the "word-salads" coming out of it would ever lead one to suspect: "Fragmentary and otherwise disturbed associations may render the speech of the schizophrenic illogical or even unintelligible although in the mind of the patient the ideas behind it may be connected."[40] Now language in the theatre *being* nothing but the manifestation of consciousness, "schizophrenia"—understood as the inability or refusal to manifest consciousness—is really the only thing that can go wrong with it. Prose, verse, high style, low style, speech rhythms, incantational rhythms—all can have a share in the work of manifestation. The one assumption about language which theatre cannot accept is the very one that it is being pressured on all sides—from within, by proponents of subtextual analysis; from without, by advocates of the various schizoid mind/language theories we examined—into accepting: that "when *speaks* the soul, alas, the *soul* no longer speaks";[41] that consciousness is not manifested, but betrayed or buried in an act of speech.

It is often argued that the decline of language in our theatre is more than compensated for by the resurgence of more specifically *theatrical* modes of expression: stage metaphor, design practices, mime, and so on. But the very distinction between language and other means of dramatic expression is spurious—never mind the question of which is the more "theatrical." What place have they, any of them, in the theatre, but as modes of hierophany? None of them was born in the theatre; none can advance a claim of birth. They are all "of" the theatre only insofar as they can bring some aspect of the *illud tempus* among us. Consequently, loss of faith in what any of them do is a symptom of a nascent mistrust of what they all do; and must inevitably be followed by loss of faith in all the rest. What is really crumbling, in such a case, is confidence in the ability of *any* exterior channel to manifest the life of the Image—confidence, that is to say, in the possibility of the theatrical event itself. Our theatre's problem with language, in other words, is a problem with more than language.

Why, however, should language be the first to go? Here, too, the analogy (I should like to think it is only an analogy) with schizophrenia can be of help.

I have labelled the status of language in our theatre "schizophrenic" on the grounds that the divorce between consciousness and expression which we find there is also an early symptom of schizophrenic sickness. But it is only an *early* symptom; it is not, as in aphasia, the whole extent of the disease. There soon develops a far more comprehensive rupture between mental and bodily life, of which that between consciousness and expression is seen in retrospect to have been only the harbinger:

> The individual's being is cleft in two, producing a disembodied self and a body that is a thing that the self looks at, regarding it at times as though it were just another thing in the world. The total body and also many 'mental' processes are severed from the self, which may continue to operate in a very restricted enclave (phantasying and observing), or it may appear to cease to function altogether (i. e. be dead, murdered, stolen).[42]

Schizophrenic persons who at first show only linguistic symptoms soon begin to act out the deeper split implicit in those symptoms between their physical bodies and "real" (i. e., disembodied) selves. So, the following example suggests, do schizophrenic theatre movements:

> "The Odets Kitchen" was an investigation into the reality behind surface behavior. Jean-Claude van Itallie, at the time a new writer and a member of Chaikin's workshop, wrote a short scene in the manner of the naturalistic play-

wrights. (It was named for Odets, but Chayevsky, Miller or Inge would have done as well.) A mother, father and daughter are stuck in their tiny New York apartment on a rainy day. Mother irons, father watches TV, and daughter mopes. To begin with, three actors simply performed the script, which was labelled the "outside."

Then, using the vocabulary of sound-and-movement, the same three actors improvised what they imagined to have been going on *behind* the external behavior of the three characters, but which the naturalistic mode of presentation had not made visible. They abstracted from the outside, distilled and explored the inner life of the given situation, looking for the characters' private miseries or fantasies and for the tensions or harmonies of the characters' relationships. The material could be closely related to what had occurred on the outside or it could be entirely divorced from it, depending on what the actors felt—not thought—to be relevant. This was called the "inside." After it, the actors performed the outside again.[43]

Here the always potentially schizoid split between text and subtext is allowed to blossom on the stage in its full schizoid form as a total dissociation between physical and mental life. As language is not the only channel by which consciousness is manifested, it cannot remain the only channel to be affected by a deepening mistrust of the basic premise of manifestation: that the mental can *be present* in the physical. If the body is not thought of as conjoined to the self but rather as "just another thing in the world," how can the body manifest those aspects of the self by which the hungan-actor might make an Image present? A theatre that begins with a schizoid view of relations between language and consciousness will soon be making schizoid refusals of its other means of manifestation as well.

The schizoid person is not only skeptical of the possibility of manifestation, he actively fears it:

> The person whom we call 'schizoid' feels both more exposed, more vulnerable to others than we do, and more isolated. Thus a schizophrenic may say that he is made of

glass, of such transparency and fragility that a look directed at him splinters him to bits and penetrates straight through
him.[44]

That is, he regards himself as *all too manifest* already. Far
from seeking involvement in a process that brings mental
impulses to the surface, his ideal is *"never to give himself
away to others."*[45] Where the hungan-actor seeks to bring
about possession of his body by elements of his self (those
elements which he holds in common with the Image), the
schizophrenic scorns—and fears—to acknowledge a connection between his self and his body.

In short, schizophrenia is the very antithesis of acting—
the ultimate atrophy of those faculties of which acting represents the ultimate development. No wonder that Grotowski, who believes that "civilization is sick with schizophrenia, which is a rupture between . . . body and soul,"[46]
defines actor-training as the closing of whatever schizoid
gap between mental and physical may be present in the
student: "The education of an actor in our theatre is not a
matter of teaching him something; we attempt to eliminate
his organism's resistance to [his] psychic process. The result
is freedom from time-lapse between inner impulse and
outer reaction."[47]

A schizophrenic patient once scrawled on the wall of his
asylum: "God is within me. So there."[48] Nothing could be
further from the actor's earnest commitment to make the
god within *him*—the possessing Image—show through his
every gesture and word. A theatre that takes as its motto
"God is within me. So there" will soon be no more inclined
to put its bodies at the Image's disposal than at present it
puts its words. The question of whether theatre should be
"verbal" or "physical" is a red herring. The only real question is whether *any* manifestation of "inner impulse" by
"outer reaction" will continue available to a culture already
beginning to doubt this possibility in regard to words. If

not, then the basic premise of the theatrical event—that imaginative life can be made present—is in doubt; and the doubt falls as heavily on the most physical as on the most verbal theatre style.

It has been said of the Hebrew prophet that he regarded his entire person as the "mouth" of God.[49] At the opposite extreme from this attitude, a character in a recent play describes himself as suffering from "lockjaw . . . all over."[50] Here are precisely the alternatives between which theatre must ultimately decide. The choice is whether to develop "lockjaw all over" or to become "all mouth."

CHAPTER 6

"Interpretation"

OURS is a theatre characterized by unwillingness to accept the kind of event theatre is. I have already presented some evidence for this in my discussion of dramatic language and, earlier, of audience participation. In each of these areas, practices which seemed to promise a renewal of theatre were shown to be, ultimately, a refusal of it. This final chapter will be devoted to an analysis of what is perhaps the most pervasive of these refusals masked as renewals: a set of related tendencies to which I give the name "interpretation."

The argument of the chapter can be very briefly stated. Theatre is an offer of participation in a universal—or at any rate, a larger than personal—way of seeing. By "interpretation," I mean the refusal, on some basis, of this offer. Both audiences and theatre practitioners can make such a refusal; their reasons for doing so are to some extent the same, to some extent a product of the different pressures that confront a spectator and a performer. Since theatre's ability to extend such an offer follows directly from the kind of event theatre is, the refusal of that offer—"interpretation"—is ultimately a refusal of the theatrical event itself.

As in my discussions of audience participation and dramatic language, I shall not limit myself to criticizing what seem to me destructive tendencies. I shall also try, in each case, to suggest at least the general lines of a more fruitful approach..

In what sense is theatre an offer of participation in a universal way of seeing?

That theatre should be widely and instantly comprehensible is not wishful thinking; it follows from the nature of the event. "Hierophany" is total revelation; being a hierophany, theatre totally reveals. To say this is no more than to repeat the definition of theatre we have been working with. A manifestation cannot but be *manifest*.

Theatre is the art of the self-evident, of what everybody knows—the place where *things mean what they sound and look like they mean*. It never makes a new or unwarranted connection (though it may demand that we be more than usually alert about recognizing a connection it points to). It demands only our having gained some sense of what in experience goes with what: that is, what gestures, movements, expressions, and tones tend to arise in what life situations— and can therefore manifest them. Since "life situations" can include (as well as social and personal relations) the natural world, introspection, nightmare, and fantasy, the theatregoer is expected to have quite a range of experiences to bring to bear, but nothing beyond what any human being acquires simply by participating in the shared experience of the race.

Whether at its most wildly surreal or its most staidly realistic, theatre asks of its audience nothing more than the ability to recognize images so universal and immediate that it would try ingenuity to find a disguise for them. Agamemnon's tread upon purple; Ranevskaya's childhood house; Feydeau's world of banging doors; the half-hidden spirits of the Noh; Everyman going a journey and Estragon going nowhere; Strindberg's skeleton in the closet and Ionesco's corpse on the stair; the Poland of Ubu, the seacoast of Bo-

hemia; Phèdre's labyrinth and Solness's tower—the faculty
by which we understand such images is the same that enables us to associate misery with darkness, sunrise with
promise, and horizons with the unknown; to see perfection
in a circle, menace in a shadow, and degradation in a pit;
to identify a hand raised in anger or the lift of an angry
voice. We recognize the images which the theatre depends
upon our recognizing because to be human is to recognize
them.

By "images" in the present context I mean something
very like what Jung called the "eternal archetypes." I call
these by a word I have already employed earlier in another
sense (and with a capital *i*) because, even at the risk of ter-
minological confusion, I wish to emphasize the suitability
of theatre's resources to theatre's aim. Because it craves to
be manifest to all, an "Image" chooses an art of universal
"images" by which to manifest itself. Because it is an art of
universal "images," theatre can provide an "Image" with
means of manifestation on a scale with its craving.

The great value of the archetypes, according to Jung,
is the relief they provide from the isolation of merely personal consciousness:

> For example, the individual is no longer confronted with
> his own mother, but with the archetype of the "maternal";
> no longer with the unique personal problem created by his
> own mother as a concrete reality, but with the universally
> human, impersonal problem of everyman's dealings with
> the primordial maternal ground in himself. Anyone who has
> ever been through such a psychic experience knows what
> an immense relief this can be, how much more bearable, for
> example, it is for a son to conceive the son-father problem
> no longer on the plane of individual guilt—in relation, for
> example, to his own desire for his father's death, his agres-
> sions and desires for revenge—but as a problem of deliver-
> ance from the father, i. e., from a dominant principle of
> consciousness, that is no longer adequate for the son: a
> problem that concerns all men and has been disclosed in
> the myths and fairy tales as the slaying of the reigning old
> king and the son's accession to his throne.[1]

In that they reveal larger-than-personal patterns within which personal experience can be comprehended, the archetypes extend the offer of a way of seeing that, without devaluing individual perception, goes beyond it. Because theatre employs images that are, in breadth of reference, archetypal, a theatre performance can become the occasion of extending that offer. It may not at first be apparent why such an offer should ever be refused.

The refusal, as was noted earlier, can come either from those who make theatre or from those who witness it. I shall first consider the motives and methods of such a refusal on the part of an audience.

We must begin by recognizing that, while "relief from the isolation of personal consciousness" may sound like a fine thing, to many people in a society like ours it is bound to be felt as a threat—and felt most intensely as a threat by those who could profit most from it: I mean the type of person who regards isolation within his own consciousness as inescapable. For such a person, to be brought face to face with an archetypal image is to be brought face to face with a terrible realization. By forcing him to recognize the existence of a universality in which he cannot share, the archetypal image at one stroke confirms the fact of his isolation and shatters the delusion by which he has been able to sustain it—namely, that there was nothing universal to be missing out on anyway. Naturally, his instinct is to insulate himself against so devastating a realization. He must find a way of denying this universality that threatens him; he has an *active need* to misunderstand—and of that need, the impulse to interpret is born.

Such a need a person confidently at one with his society rarely feels. This fact can help us understand an often noted, but generally misunderstood, aspect of the relation between theatre and society. One can think of exceptions, but on the whole, great epochs in the theatre have tended to coincide with periods of great cultural cohesiveness, as, for example, in Periclean Athens, Renaissance England, and seventeenth-century France. The implication is that sharing a world-picture somehow benefits the theatrical experience of those who share it. But why should this be so? Because, it is customary to answer, theatre is freer to have significance in an atmosphere where there is some measure of agreement on what is significant. But there can be no "more" or "less" in theatre's way of having significançe. "In the most elementary hierophany," writes Mircea Eliade, "*everything is declared.*"[2] Is it, then, that more cohesive societies produce more perceptive audiences? But as we saw in Chapter 3, the mere situation of having been "rounded upon" is sufficient to awaken in *any* audience whatever perceptual abilities they will be needing.[3] Membership in a cohesive society confers no special powers on a spectator. It only ensures that there will be nothing frightening to him in the *idea* of a universal image; that he will have no stake in denying the *possibility* of an image's being universal. On the contrary, the very tendency of his society to concur (whatever beliefs it concurs in) inclines him to regard significance as universally apparent —the ideal frame of mind for experiencing an art whose significances *are* universally apparent. Whatever the sources of his society's cohesion, his resting secure in it leaves his mind open to things meaning what they look like they mean.

And conversely—returning to the situation of the contemporary audience member—an unshakable conviction of isolation, whatever *its* source, produces a compulsion to deny self-evidence, to refute the existence of a refuge that lies open before you—in short, to interpret.

The interpreter's first step must be to conceal from himself his own role in initiating the interpretative process. This he does by projecting his own refusal of intelligibility onto the image: he declares the proceedings "obscure." Now a poem or a novel or a painting may very well be obscure, but, as we have seen, the very nature of hierophany rules out that possibility for a theatrical event. The theatre, one might almost say, would not know how to be obscure if it tried.

The interpreter, however, has resolved on bewilderment, and will not be gainsaid. He alleges obscurity on the grounds that an image may well be a blend of strange, incongruous elements, like the devil-horse in Cocteau's *Orphée*. Of course, in such cases it is the resultant blend of strange, incongruous responses that the image was constructed to evoke. Such images are the furthest thing from obscurities: they clearly mean their ambivalence. Godot, for example, "means" neither welfare capitalism nor God, but the maddening inadequacy of the assurances people live by; means, that is to say, exactly what he seems to mean. We must learn to trust the direction in which an image points us, and not demand foursquareness when we are fortunate enough to have been put in the way of a mystery. Anyway, are we so accustomed to receiving instant enlightenment in all other areas of experience that we will settle for nothing less from the stage? The theatre has not always understood, either; and how better than by images of ambivalence can this be conveyed? But even when the images cry their meaning forth, the interpreter sits poring over them like a cryptographer laboring to crack a sentence which only his determination to believe that all meaning is coded keeps him from recognizing as plain English. In short, the audience that declares theatre to be "obscure" has not made a statement about theatre, but about itself.

The capacity of archetypal images to speak for themselves having been denied, the way is clear for advancing the fundamental interpretative claim: "This thing can have meaning only insofar as I consent to give it a place in the constellation of my concerns." Not only is the image's offer of a larger-than-personal significance declined, the image is declared to be dependent on individuals for any significance at all.

The interpreter passes from a recipient to a bestower of significance in one of two ways. The first is made possible by the fact that archetypal images are bound to be suggestive on a number of levels:

The "archetype of the maternal," for example, is pregnant with all the aspects and variations in which "motherliness" can manifest itself, e. g., the sheltering cave, the belly of the whale, the womb of the church, the helpful fairy or wicked witch, the ancestress, the Magna Mater, or (on the level of individual life) one's own personal mother.[4]

The interpreter can use this very breadth of reference in the image to deny the image breadth of reference. That is, he can diminish the image by identifying it as a whole with some one of the meanings it includes—whichever one happens to interest him. So at a performance of *Waiting for Godot*, for example, Pozzo and Lucky come to stand as ciphers for Capital and Labor, the System and the Individual, Money and Art, or whatever else happens to be on somebody's mind at the moment. An archetypal image making its way across such an audience is like a great river dissipating itself among a thousand rills.

For those too proud to accept anything from an image, even a meaning they have had an opportunity of tailoring to their own limitations, there is another approach that by-passes the image altogether. This might be called interpretation by preemptive strike: before the image can have an opportunity to inflict its meaning, the interpreter dispatches some wholly irrelevant preoccupation of his own to penetrate and neutralize it. This is a type of interpretation that is much in favor with activists of all persuasions. For certainly it is more active-minded to send out "jamming" signals of one's own than to be a perfect receptor of the theatre's emissions. And therefore we cannot do interpreting enough to please a Brecht or a Julian Beck. "Don't just sit there registering it all like a barometer," scolds *der Boss*, "use your mind!"; whereas not even the intensest mental activity, if merely mental, will win an approving nod from the bonzes of the Living.

The tendency of contemporary audiences to inflict preemptive strikes receives powerful negative reinforcement from their television-watching and movie-going experience. For in contrast with television and film, where the viewer's eye is dragged around by the scruff of the neck to share another man's perspective, the theatre, for many, has come to seem the unique refuge of *the eye that chooses for itself* when to zoom, where to pan, what to watch. After long hours of viewing film or television, an audience member feels, upon entering a theatre, such elation at being perceptually on his own again that he is likely to treat the whole experience as an exercise in self-assertion—with, of course, the noisy approval of the theatre itself, which would roast its grandmother to reclaim the audiences of the silver and home screens.

Thus theatre audiences are encouraged on all sides to make exactly the wrong kind of effort—and to congratulate themselves on having made it. But far from needing to unlearn a shameful passivity, audiences have not learned to be anywhere near passive enough. Brecht's complaint that people do not *think* in the theatre is unhappily out of date: in terror of what any deeper response to archetypal images might show them about themselves, they now do little else.

I turn now to the motives and methods which practitioners, as distinguished from spectators, of the theatrical event find for enacting their refusal of theatre's offer of universality. "Practitioners" here means primarily directors, but can include actors and designers to the extent that these persons are allowed autonomy in their work on a production.

Those who make theatre can turn from a universal image for all the same reasons, and in all the same ways, as those who attend theatre. They are, after all, members of the same society as their audiences; they, too, are likely to feel isolated and threatened by a universality in which they cannot share.

But by virtue of their more active role, they possess an opportunity which mere onlookers do not: they can stamp the character of their refusal on the theatrical event itself. This they do (1) by offering their "jamming" of a universal image as, itself, a performance, and (2) by forcing universal images to serve some extratheatrical purpose which narrows their range of suggestiveness. (1) and (2) clearly do not exclude each other; in fact, they are rarely found apart. I will, however, consider them one at a time.

The first way in which a theatre practitioner can enact his refusal of universal images is to mount a production in which his "jamming" of the script is itself offered as the theatrical event. I am referring to those so-called "concept" productions, in which a play is staged in such a way as to subvert its original values or at least reorder its original emphases. The Peter Brook productions of *King Lear* and *A Midsummer Night's Dream* are well known recent examples of this phenomenon. (The phenomenon itself is far from recent, however, dating back at least to Meyerhold's productions in the twenties and, arguably, to Lugné-Poe's symbolist stagings of Ibsen thirty years before that.)

Concept productions are essentially acts of criticism—"directorial essays," in Robert Brustein's phrase[5]—not only in the obvious sense that they are often inspired by specific critical writings (as the Peter Brook *Lear* was inspired by the *Lear* chapter of Jan Kott), but in the far more fundamental sense that they themselves tend to be staged enactments of the process of critical thinking.

Take, for example, one of the earliest and best concept productions, Meyerhold's version of *The Inspector General*.[6] When Meyerhold incorporated passages from Gogol's novels and notebooks into the script, was he not employing the critical technique of using an author's other works to illuminate the text at hand? When Meyerhold changed the setting of the play from an insignificant provincial town to St. Petersburg, was he not enacting the sympathetic critic's claim of "broader significance" for a work commonly undervalued? When Meyerhold arranged the stage as a

Figure 3: V. E. Meyerhold's production of Gogol's *The Inspector General*, Moscow, 1926. *Courtesy of Theatre Collection, The New York City Public Library at Lincoln Center; Astor, Lenox and Tilden Foundations.*

semicircle of doors through which characters pop in and depart as needed (*Figure 3*), was he not building onstage a model of the way characters are present in a critic's mind—on hand, to be "admitted" or "left out," as the discussion requires? And finally, does not the famous ending (in which the actors froze in tableau and were replaced, under a blackout, by mannequins) display—or perhaps parody—the critic's confidence that he has "fixed the significance" of the work once and for all?

Again, Grotowski's whole theatre of "confronted" texts is one vast staging of the critical act:

> We eliminate those parts of the text which have no significance for us, those parts with which we can neither agree nor disagree. Within the montage one finds certain words that function *vis-à-vis* our own experiences.[7]

"Eliminate those parts of the text which have no significance," "find certain words that function"—it is not clear whether we are reading a director's description of his preparatory work on a production, or a critic's account of his preliminary research for an article.

In the concept production, themes and patterns of the script are made physically present on the stage in the form of production elements (patterns of light and movement, objects, units of space). The physical arrangement and manipulation of these elements then becomes a *staged critical investigation* of the themes and patterns for which the elements stand. In a recent concept version of *Oedipus Rex*, for example—John Perreault's *OEDIPUS, A New Work*[8]— the script motif of self-awareness is made physically present onstage in the form of a large mirror. Then the basic "two in one" pattern of experience in the play (Oedipus and Laius meeting in Jocasta, Oedipus and his children originating from Jocasta, two highways meeting at a crossroads, the two sexes meeting in Tiresias) is made physically present onstage in the form of a visual pattern: a huge tape Y on the floor. Moving the mirror into different positions with respect to the tape pattern thus becomes a way for the actor playing Oedipus to explore different possible relations between the script motifs for which mirror and tape Y respectively stand: individual consciousness and tragic pattern (*Figure 4*).

The concept production represents the triumph of the late nineteenth-century and early twentieth-century campaign to establish the director as the central organizing imagination in the theatre. There is, of course, a certain irony in Reinhardt's and Craig's dream of the director-as-supercreator having issued in works of staged criticism. But it is a facile irony, and we would do well not to press it. The example of such figures as Valéry, Pound, and Mann should long since have taught us to distrust a simple distinction between critical and creative activity. The trouble with theatre's turning into criticism is not that it thereby ceases to be creative, but that, as we shall presently see, it thereby ceases to provide audiences with what they come to theatre for.

Figure 4: John Perreault's production of his *OEDIPUS: A New Work*, New York City, 1971. *Photograph by Michael Kirby.*

Nor is the quality of the criticism which concept productions offer really the issue. One might be inclined to suppose that a production could be no better than the critical insight informing it, but that is not necessarily the case. An expressionist *Hamlet* or *The Merchant of Venice* in Auschwitz may not be fully satisfactory manifestations of their

Images, but each brings out some facet of the *illud tempus* in question which a more balanced manifestation, precisely because it *was* more balanced, would not. The problem with concept productions is not with the quality of their criticism, but with their *being* criticism. For theatre performance and critical exegesis have different goals, neither of which can be achieved if the two activities are compressed into a single event.

Concept productions are often praised for "translating" a remote *illud tempus* "into our terms." While this is a legitimate aim for criticism, it is not at all the objective of theatre. Theatre does all the "translating into our terms" it should ever want to do when it translates imaginative noumena into human presences. Criticism exists to help us find a common ground with strangeness; but theatre exists to provide the strangeness, so that we may have an opportunity of seeking common ground with it. If theatre takes for its own the critical task of palliating strangeness—where are we to go for the experience of strangeness itself?

Like audience participation, the concept production is an attempt to revitalize the theatrical event by means which in fact abolish it. For whereas theatre encourages encounter with what is other, the concept production, by its identification of what is other with what is familiar, encourages an audience to stay with what it knows. The Perreault *OEDIPUS*, for example, "translates" *Oedipus Rex* "into our terms" by providing homely "equivalents" for the characters, incidents, and motifs of Sophocles's play. The oracle is represented by an I Ching casting; the Sphinx's riddle, by a riddle-book; Queen Jocasta, by a photograph of the main actor's mother; the Messenger's narrative, by a slide show, and so on. Instead of offering contact with otherness, such a production offers assurances that otherness need not be encountered—seeing that our own milieu provides such ready analogues for everything that might at first be supposed "other." To experience this *illud tempus*, the spectator is made to feel, nothing more is required than to experience his own usual preoccupations. And how much more comfortable one always is with a preoccupation—even the grimmest—that happens to be one's own or one's age's own. So we get *The Bacchae* as a police-freak confrontation, *Love's Labours Lost* in psychedelic drag, and in general whatever is implacably strange as reassuringly familiar. Call this "finding relevance" if you will; in fact, it is the gambit of men afraid of what they might find, and trying to arrange an affinity on their own terms. Interpretation, which originates in the attempt to defend against feelings of isolation, ends by confirming them. For the experience of strangeness has been substituted the experience of self.

A concept production is thus a director's version of that process of "jamming" which we have already considered as an audience response. But with this difference: that here the audience is deprived even of the opportunity to do its own jamming. The director has been out and done it for them— and now presents his record of that experience *as the show*. In lieu of an encounter, the audience is offered the role of a witness at someone else's. But since theatre exists precisely to enable *each* of us to have that encounter, such a substitution deprives an audience of the very thing theatre exists to provide.

Have we any real alternative to a theatre of concept productions? Does it come down to a choice between that and a theatre of waxwork recreations? Surely neither of these possibilities is acceptable. What is wanted is neither lifeless shamming of earlier performance styles nor a redefinition of theatre as a staging of the difficulties one experiences in trying to recover them, but rather *rearrival* at the old style by the same course of rehearsal experimentation that brought it into being as a style in the first place; in other words, exploration of unknown routes to the known; in other words, shamanic quest.

A performance tradition dies when it ceases to be understood as an outcome. What Hegel said about works of philosophy also applies to styles in art: "The result [is not] the actual whole, but only the result together with its becoming. . . . the naked result is the corpse which has left the tendency behind."[9] An old-fashioned (but still available) acting manual like Chisman and Raven-Hart's *Manners and Movements in Costume Plays* provides instance after instance of such corpselike "naked results" which have "left the tendency behind." Here, for example, is an excerpt from the section on period bows:

> EIGHTEENTH CENTURY.
> *On entering a room—en avant.*
> Pause on last step of entering (which may be left foot) right foot slightly to the side, heel somewhat raised, toe pressing lightly on floor, knee straight; bend body and scrape open foot in one entire motion inwards, bending the knee of the left leg; pause for a minute, arms hanging naturally from shoulders. Rise erect on scraping foot, other falling into Ist position (heels together) ready to repeat.[10]

That is all: no thought given to what attitudes toward the body and social relations these movements may have been the expression of; or to how these particular movements ever evolved into the accepted expression of them. To follow such instructions is not to act; it is, literally, to go through the motions of an *illud tempus* one has not sought to make present.

Many contemporary theatre practitioners have recognized as much—and have responded by mounting concept productions. And yet there is no reason why, on discovering that, say, a certain pattern of movement has become meaningless, one's next step should be to cast about for some contemporary "equivalent" to replace it with. The objection, after all, is not to the pattern of movement, but to its meaninglessness. Having flung the rote-manual aside with a shudder, one must take it up again with a question: What has been the *process* of stylization, of which I am now being asked to adopt the outcome? A solution that we have not

reached can become our solution—provided we are willing
to go through the experience of reaching it:

> When the living traditions of a great art have been destroyed,
> the . . . imitation of its products will lead no farther to-
> wards creation than the naïve imitation of nature. A reviving
> art must begin at the beginning, and endeavour to penetrate
> step by step into the secrets of art construction.[11]

Bernard Berenson is here discussing the encounter of the
Renaissance painter with the art of classical antiquity. But
the highly shamanic vein of his imagery ("penetrates step by
step into the secrets . . .") suggests that his remarks also have
an application to theatre. An old theatre style is a destination:
we know *what* it is; what we don't know is how to get there.
But to have recognized it as a destination is simultaneously
to have discovered a method of recovery. An imaginative
destination can only be reached by that journey in imagination which is the specialty of the shaman and of the actor-
as-shaman. A theatre company's way to an old performance
style is by the same road an actor takes to the *illud tempus*;
indeed, the conventions of movement and gesture which constitute a performance style figured in our original definition
of what a script *illud tempus* might be. A theatre company
will never live in a style until they have relived the evolution of the style; they must "get to be that way" by experiencing how the style "got to be that way." Just as the actor
rediscovers aspects of the Image as potentialities in himself,
so they must rediscover aspects of the style as potentialities
of expression in themselves. The model for reanimating a
style is animating a role.

I spoke earlier of *two* ways a contemporary theatre practitioner can enact his refusal of the universal images in which
theatre deals. Having discussed the first of these, the concept production, I turn now to the second: the imposition
of extratheatrical "purpose" on theatrical activity. Here, as
with the concept production, I shall first offer a critique of

prevailing attitudes, and then go on to suggest a perspective on the problem more in accord with the nature of the theatrical event.

Any attempt to make theatre serve an extraneous purpose diminishes the universal images by which theatre expresses itself; for only the aspect of the image relevant to that purpose can now be acknowledged to be present. But more is sacrificed in such cases than the scope of individual images. The desire to give theatre a purpose is a refusal of what theatre gives—of the theatrical event itself.

Theatre exists to manifest an *illud tempus*. All theatre that exists—or thinks it does—to do something else, I call "political theatre," irrespective of what the something else is. Theatre that strives to convince us of the labor theory of value is obviously political, but theatre that longs to liberate our consciousness or feast our senses is no less so. Street plays and cabaret, of course, fall into this category; but so also do the productions of the playwrights as thinkers and the purveyors of "overwhelming experiences." To want to knock an audience on its ear is to want to do something to them—a purpose like any other.

For it is not a question of this or that purpose being unsuitable. The mistake lies in envisioning theatre as a thing for which a purpose must be found. Theatre does not *serve* purposes; it *has* a purpose: to bring us the presence of imaginative events. The idea that theatre can have purpose "given" to it is like the idea of someone sitting down to give purpose to the telephone. The telephone is only there before him as a solution to a specific problem: how to make voices audible at a distance. There is no question of having to find something for it to be after the fact.

If someone *does* attempt to make theatre serve an extraneous purpose, theatre initiates a subtle resistance. It offers no overt opposition, but instead sets about rechannelling the energies and resources that are being siphoned off from it back to its own use. We see this in the fine moment at the end of *The Good Woman of Setzuan* when the water-carrier Wang turns from the play's distressing denouement to address the audience:

> Ladies and gentlemen, don't be angry! Please!
> We know the play is still in need of mending
>
> . . .
>
> *We're* disappointed too. With consternation
> We see the curtain closed, the plot unended.
> In your opinion, then, what's to be done?
> Change human nature or—the world? Well: which?
> [Brecht, *The Good Woman of Setzuan*][12]

The upshot of this attempt to increase our political awareness by means of the theatrical event is to increase our awareness of the theatrical event. We are set thinking, all right, but hardly about whether to "change human nature or the world." The audacity and rightness of the speech itself, and of such an ending, are the topic to which our thoughts turn. Here, as so often with political theatre, the invitation-to-consider is really an invitation to consider the ingenuity of the means the playwright has found of issuing the invitation.

The tendency of theatre to turn others' purposefulness to its own purpose can also be observed in the case of those "striking parallels" which political dramatists are so fond of introducing into their works, on the assumption that you can get a better understanding of Europe's drift toward war in the thirties if you see it dramatized as Troy's drift toward war with Greece (Giraudoux's *The Trojan War Will Not Take Place*); of political witch-hunts if you see them dramatized as actual witch-hunts (Miller's *The Crucible*); of German fascists, if you see them dramatized as Chicago gangsters (Brecht's *The Preventable Rise of Arturo Ui*); and so forth. Now again, it is quite true, as proponents of the technique claim, that such parallels "make you think"; but again our question must be: about what? Surely it is not the real-life event being paralleled that invites reflection so much as the working-out of the parallel itself. Now as long as you are busy deciding: *from what I know about the rise of the*

Nazis, how telling a parallel do these Chicago events make to it?, the one aspect of the question it will *not* occur to you to re-think is your position on the rise of the Nazis. You need your preconception in that area as a standard against which to judge the appropriateness of the developing parallel. Thus the very point which the parallel was introduced in the hope of getting you to re-examine must go unexamined if the parallel is to function. Not only can such a device not change your preconception, your preconception is indispensable to it.

Not every political play proceeds by parallels. But the same self-defeat which that technique brings upon itself awaits any attempt to "dramatize" a problem. Confronted with a problem, one considers the problem. Confronted with a dramatization of a problem, one's attention is diverted (as, one usually feels, the playwright's has been) from problem to dramatization. The "rounding" claims for itself all the interest it generates; any attempt to make theatre political leads straight back to what is sneeringly known as "formalism" (i. e., staying open to the Image's demands). Nowhere do we see this more clearly than in the case of Brecht himself, who, as his Stalinist critics rightly pointed out, was the all-time formalist in didact's clothing. The whole purpose of his style, he maintained, was to encourage political judgment. But the very devices necessary to achieve the style— song, verse, caricature, mask—work to remove the plays from the class of activities to which political judgment seems an appropriate response.

But, of course, far more than our *judgments* on extra-theatrical matters, it is our *feelings* toward them that political theatre hopes to influence. And here, too, all it *does* influence is our experience of the theatrical means it employs to this end—the theatrical means being, in this case, empathy.

There is a school of ethical thought that regards empathy as the source of our moral feelings, on the assumption that to be capable of imagining an evil is to be incapable of committing it; so that, as Shelley put it, "the great instrument of moral good is the imagination."[13] This seems to me a spectacularly unborne-out assumption, not instantly recognizable as such only because it provides such a flattering way of accounting for our good impulses. To have been virtuous is also to have been imaginative—what a bonus! However, it is not the general truth or falsehood of the proposition which concerns me. My point is that even if empathic feeling could guarantee behavior, it would be absurd to expect this result from the mere *impression* of empathy which theatre produces for its own purposes, as it produces the impression of years passing or outdoor light. The empathic responses stirred in us by an Image hungry for attentiveness can only return upon the Image—have only been produced to that end. Indeed, all feeling that theatre creates can only go back into the theatre, can no more be *our* feeling than a painted flat can be our landscape. What does it say for us that we even think of drawing our feelings from such a source! It is a symptom of something art cannot cure when a society begins looking to art for cures.

But never mind extraneous, superadded "purposes." I wonder if even the legitimate purpose of theatre—to bring audiences into the presence of an alternative reality—does not get to looking rather sinister when scrutinized for political overtones. A few years ago we had a popular art/theatre form called the "environment." "Environments" were tunnel-of-love-like chambers through which audiences were conducted so as to experience a sequence of visual and auditory stimuli that somebody had laid out for them. Considered from a political point of view, must not any theatre performance be seen as, implicitly, what an "environment" explicitly was—an attempt to structure and control the reality through which others (the audience) must pass? Is this a construction we would be happy to have put on our theatre-making? Does it imply a political stance which those who are most anxious to see theatre politicized would wish to be associated with?

Of course, "environments"—and one could affirm this even more confidently of conventional theatre-forms—are only *fantasies* of social engineering, in the grand tradition of ornamental ruins and landscaped wildernesses. But is a regimentarian impulse any less disturbing for contenting itself with fantasies of regimentation? This is only to impugn the seriousness of theatre's intentions without rescuing their character. A dictated reality is the political event of which theatre must be regarded as having the form—if it is to be regarded as a political event at all. But the tendency to regard it in that way is already a misunderstanding. If theatre has any political dimension, it is not by virtue of treating political themes or curing political ills, but because it provides one of the few ways we have left of experiencing a sense of community—the shared, common plight of the rounded upon. But this *sense* of community, born of and limited in duration to the theatrical event, must not be mistaken for an actual community that can be taken out of the theatre and lived. In general, we must be careful not to confuse what the Image creates for its own needs with what we would like to create for ours. The theatre has all it can do to make its own miracles; it cannot also make society's.

It is a measure of how encrusted with "interpretative" attitudes theatrical activity in our culture has become, that the preceding remarks appear paradoxical and startling. For so long now has theatre been engaged in doing other people's business that we have almost forgotten it has a business of its own to do.

In the hope of offering a corrective to this state of affairs, I put forward the following set of propositions. They are, I suppose, half-truths; but I make no apology for them on that account. A half-truth can often illuminate by the very glare of its inadequacy; and besides, the assumptions which these half-truths challenge are too deep-seated to be shaken by polite qualification. Here they are, then—and I would own to worse, if I thought it would help:

Theatre on Theatre

Theatre has only one subject matter, not theatre's to choose, but inherent in the kind of event theatre is. A given work of theatre can only be about what theatre itself is about: the manifestation of an *illud tempus*. There are not "thirty-six dramatic situations," but one: an Image would be present.

Wittgenstein made us aware that philosophy is not, as had been traditionally supposed, thinking about one subject or another; it is thinking about thinking. Similarly, theatre is not, as has been traditionally supposed, mimesis of one subject or another, but the art that takes as its subject the paradoxes of mimesis.

Theatre has mimesis, not as its method, but as its subject matter.

There is no place in the theatre for the great concerns of man: suffering, identity, justice, love, death. Theatre is not about the problems of man; it is about the problems of its own realization. Of course, theatre must be about something *in the course* of being about its own realization —nor is the "something" a matter of indifference. A playwright looks for the situation which provides the best and most opportunities for exploring the mimetic problem that interests him. But it *is* the mimetic problem that interests him; the situation is only a means. Nothing matters more to the theatre than the theatre. A playwright does not solve a technical problem on the way to dramatizing something else; he takes the something else as an occasion for dramatizing the solution of the technical problem.

Theatre holds the mirror up to nature—but only so as to be able to examine the properties of the mirror.

Theatre consists of a careful validation of its own expressive choices; the choices once validated, the performance is over.

Theatre is a staging of the dilemmas of staging. A play's crises are its own crises of expression. Obviously this is true of a play like *Six Characters in Search of an Author*; but the point is, of what play is it *not* true? Beckett's concern is with the difficulties of plenishing a stage. Ibsen and Chekhov dramatize the struggle to achieve everything within the conventions of realism. Strindberg's later plays chronicle the stage's effort to depict consciousness. Genet's one theme is mimesis. *All* theatre is "on theatre," if we can learn to see in it an opportunity for studying the difficulties an Image encounters in coming before us. *Six Characters in Search of an Author* is the story of any play. The rounding is not merely a description of theatre, it is the subject of theatre. Not what the Images are of, but how they got there, is the drama.

These are, as I say, half-truths. They are the half-truths we need.

Notes

Where only one work by an author has been used as a source, references to that work are given in the form: author and page number.

Where two or more works by an author have been used as sources, references to each work are given in the form: author, short title, page number.

Full bibliographical information on each book, play, and article cited may be found in the "List of Works Consulted," below, pp. 171-177.

Chapter 1: Theatre and the Script

1. Keats, *Ode to a Nightingale*, line 80.
2. Kasanin, pp. 126, 119.
3. Wordsworth, *The Recluse*, lines 816-824.
4. From a 1915 letter, quoted in Rilke, p. 16.
5. Laing, pp. 84-85.
6. Eliade, *Patterns*, p. 392.
7. Pirandello, p. 266.
8. Eliade, *Shamanism*, p. 103.
9. Eliade, *Sacred and Profane*, p. 86.
10. Jung, pp. 100ff.
11. Eliade, *Sacred and Profane*, p. 77 (slightly abridged).
12. Jacobi, p. 139.
13. Jacobi, p. 109.

Chapter 2: The Actor

1. See below, pp. 161-162.
2. Heusch, p. 132.
3. Charles, p. 95.
4. Eliade, *Shamanism*, p. 298.
5. Róheim, p. 234.
6. Eliade, *Shamanism*, p. 5.
7. Ibid., p. 143.
8. Ibid., p. 133.
9. Ibid., p. 143.

10. Ibid., p. 325.
11. Charles, passim; Eliade, *Shamanism*, p. 511.
12. Eliade, *Shamanism*, pp. 200-202, 309.
13. Ibid., pp. 192, 203.
14. Ibid., p. 199.
15. Ibid., pp. 196, 203.
16. Bogoras, pp. 416-417.
17. Dournes, pp. 35-36.
18. Charles, pp. 102-104; and see Eliade, *Shamanism*, pp. 145-160.
19. Charles, pp. 104-105.
20. Charles, p. 107.
21. Charles, pp. 101-102.
22. Dournes, pp. 34-35.
23. Eliade, *Shamanism*, p. 196.
24. Charles, pp. 117-118.
25. Quoted in Oesterreich, p. 301.
26. Heusch, p. 132.
27. Eliade, *Shamanism*, pp. 265-266, 487ff.
28. Ibid., p. 265.
29. Ibid., p. 103.
30. Róheim, p. 202.
31. Grotowski, p. 34.
32. Stanislavski, *Actor Prepares*, p. 237.
33. Grotowski, p. 140.
34. Spolin, p. 146.
35. *Yale/Theatre*, p. 138.
36. Stanislavski, *Actor Prepares*, p. 164.
37. Stanislavski, *Creating a Role*, p. 25.
38. Eliade, *Shamanism*, p. 5.
39. From the *Penguin Dictionary of Psychology*, quoted in Lewis, p. 38.
40. E. T. Kirby, p. 51.
41. Grotowski, pp. 37-38.
42. See below, pp. 29-31.
43. Eliade, *Shamanism*, pp. 338-339.
44. Ibid., pp. 428ff.
45. Ibid., p. 140.
46. Ibid., p. 492.
47. Stanislavski, *Actor Prepares*, pp. 51ff.
48. Ibid., p. 61.
49. Ibid., p. 43.
50. Reinhardt, p. 37.
51. *Yale/Theatre*, p. 132.
52. Eliade, *Shamanism*, pp. 156-157.
53. Ibid., p. 402.
54. Grotowski, p. 137.
55. Grotowski, p. 137.
56. Reinhardt, p. 36.
57. See, for example, Grotowski, pp. 138, 142-143; Spolin, pp. 262ff.
58. Eliade, *Shamanism*, pp. 92-93, 328-329.
59. Ibid., p. 93.
60. Ibid., pp. 200-201.
61. Stanislavski, *Creating a Role*, p. 12.
62. Eliade, *Shamanism*, pp. 234-235.
63. Stanislavski, *Actor Prepares*, p. 273.
64. Ibid., pp. 274-275.
65. Eliade, *Shamanism*, p. 182.
66. Spolin, p. 381.
67. Spolin, pp. 336-337.
68. Stanislavski, *Actor Prepares*, p. 60.
69. Ibid., pp. 90-104.
70. Eliade, *Shamanism*, pp. 53, 219-221.
71. Ibid., pp. 128, 131.
72. Blofield, pp. 83-87.

73. Eliade, *Shamanism*, p. 212.
74. Ibid., p. 201.
75. *Yale/Theatre*, p. 135.
76. Heusch, p. 138.
77. Bowers, p. 236.
78. Eliade, *Shamanism*, pp. 167-168.
79. Quoted in Oesterreich, p. 290.
80. Beattie and Middleton, p. 168.
81. Beattie and Middleton, p. 64.
82. Beattie and Middleton, p. 64.
83. Performance at the Yale University Art Gallery, March 4, 1973.
84. Leiris, p. 100. See also Oesterreich, pp. 242-243; Heusch, p. 153.
85. Leiris, p. 74.
86. Métraux, p. 413.
87. Monfouga-Nicolas, p. 156; Rouch, pp. 248-250.
88. Monfouga-Nicolas, p. 122.
89. Monfouga-Nicolas, p. 105.
90. Monfouga-Nicolas, p. 116.
91. Leiris, p. 9.
92. Beattie and Middleton, p. 51 (slightly abridged).
93. Leiris, p. 74.
94. Rouch, p. 149.
95. Bastide, *Le Candomblé*, p. 176.
96. Beattie and Middleton, p. 83.
97. Beattie and Middleton, pp. 161-162.
98. Beattie and Middleton, p. 84.
99. Beattie and Middleton, p. 84. See also Sargant, p. 139.
100. See above, pp. 18-21.
101. Leiris, pp. 48-49.
102. Leiris, pp. 26-27.
103. Métraux, p. 415.
104. Métraux, pp. 414-415.
105. Oesterreich, pp. 19-20.
106. Métraux, pp. 410, 413; Leiris, pp. 9, 34.
107. Métraux, p. 410; Monfouga-Nicolas, pp. 174-176; Beattie and Middleton, p. 86; Rouch, pp. 156-157.
108. Métraux, pp. 417, 424.
109. *Asie*, pp. 92, 94, 132 (diagram).
110. Métraux, p. 415. See also Leiris, p. 45.
111. Métraux, p. 414.
112. Monfouga-Nicolas, pp. 97-98, 275.
113. Monfouga-Nicolas, p. 271.
114. Monfouga-Nicolas, p. 271; Rouch, p. 148.
115. Monfouga-Nicolas, p. 156.
116. Rouch, pp. 192-193, 253.
117. Lewis, p. 107; Leiris, p. 62.
118. Monfouga-Nicolas, p. 153; Rouch, p. 193.
119. Bastide, *Le Rêve*, p. 95.
120. Harrison, p. 569.
121. Firth, p. 200.
122. *Asie*, p. 140.
123. Métraux, p. 409; Leiris, p. 75.
124. Oesterreich, p. 10.
125. *Yale/Theatre*, p. 132.
126. See above, p. 24.
127. Duvignaud, pp. 240, 242.
128. Louis-Jean, p. 102.
129. Stanislavski, *Actor Prepares*, p. 278.

130. Quoted in Oesterreich, p. 45. See also Métraux, p. 418.
131. Monfouga-Nicolas, p. 192.
132. Monfouga-Nicolas, p. 192.
133. Monfouga-Nicolas, pp. 289-290.
134. Quoted in Oesterreich, p. 368.
135. Quoted in Oesterreich, p. 42.
136. Monfouga-Nicolas, p. 194; Bastide, *Le Candomblé*, p. 218; Rouch, pp. 24-26; Heusch, p. 149; Métraux, p. 406.
137. Stanislavski, *Building a Character*, p. 167.
138. Freud, "A Neurosis of Demonical Possession in the Seventeenth Century," pp. 264-265.
139. Lewis, p. 181.
140. Métraux, p. 407. See also Oesterreich, pp. 125-126.
141. May, pp. 196-197.
142. May, p. 200.
143. Jung, pp. 202-203.
144. Lewis, pp. 199-200.
145. May, pp. 199-200.
146. Monfouga-Nicolas, p. 86.
147. Métraux, p. 421.
148. Grotowski, p. 16.
149. Grotowski, p. 16.
150. Stanislavski, *Building a Character*, p. 38.
151. Stanislavski, *Actor Prepares*, p. 180. Stanislavski speaks of "unconscious" rather than "repressed" feelings, but of course feelings only get to *be* unconscious by being repressed.

152. Métraux, p. 421.
153. Stanislavski, *Actor Prepares*, p. 167.
154. Rouch, pp. 73, 147.
155. Monfouga-Nicolas, pp. 97, 192-193.
156. Stanislavski, *Actor Prepares*, p. 92.
157. Grotowski, p. 16.
158. Métraux, p. 407.
159. Magarshack, p. 228.
160. Stanislavski, *Building a Character*, pp. 10-11.
161. Leiris, p. 47. See also Rouch, p. 239.
162. Monfouga-Nicolas, p. 178.
163. Stanislavski, *Actor Prepares*, p. 133.
164. Stanislavski, *Creating a Role*, p. 240.
165. Pasolli, p. 6.
166. Leiris, p. 19n.
167. Grotowski, p. 144.
168. Quoted in Oesterreich, p. 48.
169. For a thoughtful consideration of the analogy—and the limits of the analogy—between hysteria and acting, see Racamier.
170. Stanislavski, *Building a Character*, pp. 15-17.
171. Ibid., p. 19.
172. Quoted in Oesterreich, p. 29.
173. Stanislavski, *Building a Character*, p. 18.
174. Ibid., p. 19.
175. Eliade, *Shamanism*, p. 6. See also Oesterreich, p. 305.
176. Lewis, pp. 51ff.
177. Rouch, pp. 25-26.
178. *Asie*, p. 141.

179. Eliade, *Shamanism*, p. 467.
180. Métraux, p. 407.
181. Eliade, *Shamanism*, p. 487.
182. Lewis, p. 189.
183. Eliade, *Shamanism*, p. 324.
184. Róheim, pp. 178-179.

185. Eliade, *Shamanism*, pp. 452-453.
186. Ibid., p. 353.
187. Oesterreich, pp. 152-153.
188. Eliade, *Shamanism*, p. 236. See also p. 507n.
189. *Yale/Theatre*, p. 132 (slightly abridged).

Chapter 3: The Audience

1. See above, pp. 49-50.
2. Stanislavski, *Building a Character*, p. 15.
3. Ibid., pp. 15, 17.
4. Charles, p. 96.
5. May, p. 200.
6. Lewis, p. 165.
7. Métraux, p. 408.
8. Métraux, p. 410; Oesterreich, p. 262.
9. Métraux, p. 415.
10. Heusch, pp. 135-136.
11. Métraux, p. 421.
12. Leiris, p. 97.
13. *Asie*, p. 96.
14. Métraux, p. 419.
15. Métraux, pp. 411-412; Beattie and Middleton, p. 19.
16. Oesterreich, pp. 291-292.
17. Métraux, pp. 413-414.
18. Eliade, *Patterns*, p. 17.
19. Métraux, p. 417.
20. Leiris, p. 96.
21. Lewis, p. 53.
22. Rouch, p. 238.
23. Bastide, *Le Candomblé*, p. 22.
24. Louis-Jean, pp. 69-70.
25. Bowers, p. 190; Beattie and Middleton, p. 23.
26. Sargant, p. 160.
27. Freud, "The Uncanny," p. 124.

28. Freud, *Totem and Taboo*, p. 25.
29. Freud, "The Uncanny," p. 131.
30. Ibid., pp. 148, 153.
31. Ibid., pp. 155-156.
32. Ibid., p. 148.
33. Ibid., p. 152.
34. Eliade, *Patterns*, p. 15.
35. Ibid., pp. 17-18, 460.
36. Eliade, *Mephistopheles*, p. 91.
37. Freud, "A Neurosis of Demonical Possession in the Seventeenth Century," pp. 278-79. This hypothesis of Freud's is confirmed by the Gnostic myth of God and Satan as brothers—a conception which is also found in Eastern European folklore. See Eliade, *Mephistopheles*, pp. 83-84.
38. Freud, *Totem and Taboo*, pp. 29-30, 50-51.
39. Monfouga-Nicolas, p. 86.
40. Heusch, p. 167.
41. Beattie and Middleton, p. 255.
42. See above, pp. 43-45.
43. Eliade, *Patterns*, pp. 16-17.
44. Oesterreich, p. 286.

45. See, for example, the accounts of the work of Allport, Sherif, Stoner, and Asch, in Brown, pp. 656-708; and the account of the Lambert-Lowy experiments in Lambert and Lambert, p. 89. See also Luchins.
46. Freud, *Group Psychology*, p. x.
47. Ibid., p. 23.
48. Lambert and Lambert, p. 88.
49. Brown, pp. 657-663.
50. Lambert and Lambert, pp. 96-97.
51. Brown, p. 669.
52. Brown, p. 669.
53. Brown, p. 736.
54. Freud, *Group Psychology*, p. 52.
55. Ibid., p. 57.
56. Ibid., p. 61.
57. Ibid., p. 76.
58. Ibid.
59. See below, pp. 155-160.
60. Eliade, *Sacred and Profane*, pp. 86-87.
61. Carcopino, pp. 263-264.
62. Tairov, p. 137.
63. Tairov, pp. 137, 139, 149.

Chapter 4: The Scenic Means

1. Hewitt, p. 1.
2. Nicoll, pp. 62-63; Nagler, pp. 186-187.
3. See especially Book II, in Hewitt, pp. 98-177, from which many of the following examples are drawn.
4. Nagler, pp. 171-172.
5. Jonson, p. 388.
6. Jonson, p. 227.
7. Jonson, p. 228.
8. Nicoll, p. 63.
9. Hewitt, pp. 173-174.
10. Jonson, p. 96.
11. Hewitt, pp. 153-155, 175.
12. Hewitt, p. 98.
13. Hewitt, pp. 109-111.
14. Hewitt, pp. 111-113.
15. Southern, p. 187.
16. Nicoll, p. 63.
17. Arnheim, p. 287.
18. Jonson, p. 18.
19. Eliade, *Shamanism*, p. xiv.
20. Eliade, *Sacred and Profane*, pp. 40-41.
21. Jonson, p. 20.
22. Eliade, *Sacred and Profane*, pp. 11-12.
23. Eliade, *Patterns*, p. 11.
24. Eliade, *Sacred and Profane*, p. 12.
25. Monfouga-Nicolas, p. 176.
26. Eliade, *Sacred and Profane*, p. 26.
27. Ibid., p. 21.
28. Hardison, p. 51.
29. *Wisdom of Solomon* 9:8, quoted in Eliade, *Sacred and Profane*, p. 60.
30. Gaster, p. 191.
31. Bastide, *Le Candomblé*, pp. 14-15, 18, 57-59, 61.
32. Eliade, *Mephistopheles*, p. 33.
33. *Bhagavadgita*, trans. Swami Paramananda, v.

17, quoted in Eliade, *Mephistopheles*, p. 31.

34. Matthew 17:2.
35. Eliade, *Mephistopheles*, pp. 64-65.
36. Ibid., p. 51.
37. Ibid., p. 64.
38. Beattie and Middleton, p.191.
39. Douglas, p. 105.
40. Eliade, *Mephistopheles*, p. 63.
41. Exodus 34:29.
42. Exodus 34:30.
43. Pound, p. 153.
44. Pound, p. 71.
45. Maruoka and Yoshikoshi, p. 60.
46. Maruoka and Yoshikoshi, p. 31.
47. Pound, p. 26.
48. Maruoka and Yoshikoshi, pp. 100-101.
49. Pound, p. 36.
50. Eliade, *Sacred and Profane*, pp. 181-184.
51. Eliade, *Shamanism*, p. 483; *Sacred and Profane*, p. 182.
52. Pound, p. 12.
53. Eliade, *Sacred and Profane*, pp. 33-37.
54. Eliade, *Patterns*, pp. 273-278.

55. Eliade, *Sacred and Profane*, pp. 53-54.
56. Wilson, *Yeats's Iconography*, p. 28.
57. Kernodle, pp. 53-58.
58. Kernodle, p. 53.
59. The present state of scholarship in this area is summarized in Muir and Schoenbaum, pp. 15-34, and in Gurr, pp. 82-111.
60. Eliade, *Shamanism*, p. 259.
61. Eliade, *Sacred and Profane*, pp. 53-54.
62. Ibid., pp. 175-176, 178.
63. Eliade, *Shamanism*, p. 37n.
64. Eliade, *Sacred and Profane*, p. 25.
65. Róheim, pp. 56-57.
66. Berthold, p. 72.
67. Kernodle, pp. 194-195.
68. Kernodle, p. 196.
69. Eliade, *Patterns*, p. 399.
70. Wilson, *W. B. Yeats and Tradition*, pp. 232-233.
71. Charles, p. 101; Bogoras, p. 416; *Asie*, p. 13.
72. Róheim, pp. 217-218.
73. Freud, "The Uncanny," p. 161.

Chapter 5: Language

1. Ibsen, pp. 397-398.
2. Neilson and Hill, p. 317.
3. Davis, p. 345, incorporating the 1710 and 1719 variant readings given on p. 497.
4. Neilson and Hill, p. 1192.

5. Yeats, p. 430.
6. Beckett, p. 11.
7. Pinter, p. 77.
8. Synge, pp. 98-99.
9. O'Casey, p. 204.
10. Eliot, p. 133.
11. Eliot, p. 139.

12. Sokel, p. 185.
13. Michael Kirby, pp. 258-259.
14. Quoted in Esslin, p. 46.
15. Stanislavski, *Building a Character*, p. 108.
16. DeGeorge and DeGeorge, p. 91.
17. Wittgenstein, *Tractatus*, Section 4.002, p. 63.
18. Wittgenstein, *Blue Book*, p. 41.
19. Chomsky, p. 25.
20. Slobin, pp. 30-31.
21. Chomsky, p. 32.
22. Greimas, p. 14.
23. Osgood, p. 58.
24. Quoted in Slobin, p. 117.
25. Osgood, p. 265.
26. Slobin, p. 118.
27. Freud, *Psychopathology of Everyday Life*, p. 24.
28. Quoted in ibid., p. 121.
29. Ionesco, p. 24.
30. Handke, p. 85.
31. Handke, p. 85.
32. Benedikt and Wellwarth, p. 133.
33. Laing, p. 151.
34. Laing, p. 178.
35. Séchehaye, pp. 78-80.
36. Laing, p. 165.
37. Kasanin, p. 54.
38. Séchehaye, p. xiii.
39. Kasanin, p. 2.
40. Kasanin, p. x.
41. Quoted in Cassirer, p. 7.
42. Laing, p. 162.
43. Pasolli, pp. 12-13.
44. Laing, p. 37.
45. Laing, p. 71.
46. Grotowski, p. 123.
47. Grotowski, p. 16.
48. Visible in the documentary film *Asylum* (1972) by Peter Robinson.
49. Buber, p. 156.
50. Bennett, p. 12.

Chapter 6: "Interpretation"

1. Jacobi, pp. 26-27.
2. Eliade, *Shamanism*, p. xvii.
3. See above, pp. 68-69.
4. Jacobi, p. 107.
5. Brustein, p. 33.
6. See account in E. T. Kirby, pp. 145ff.
7. Quoted in Schechner, p. 180.
8. First performed at New York University on May 2, 1971. A "script/description" appears in *The Drama Review*, Vol. 15, no. 3a: T 51 (Summer 1971), pp. 141-147.
9. Hegel, p. 10.
10. Chisman and Raven-Hart, pp. 30-31.
11. Berenson, p. 53.
12. Brecht, p. 106.
13. Shelley, *A Defense of Poetry* (1821).

List of Works Consulted

This list contains bibliographical information on all works re-
ferred to by author in the notes, with the exception of the
brief quotations from Keats and Wordsworth in Chapter 1,
and from Shelley in Chapter 6.

Arnheim, Rudolph. *Art and Visual Perception: A Psychology of
the Creative Eye*. Berkeley: University of California Press,
1969.

Asie du sud-est et Monde insulindien, Vol. IV, no. 3 (1973).

Bastide, Roger. *Le Candomblé de Bahia*. Paris: Mouton, 1958.

——— . *Le Rêve, la transe et la folie*. Paris: Flammarion, 1972.

Beattie, John, and John Middleton, editors. *Spirit Mediumship
and Society in Africa*. London: Routledge & Kegan Paul, 1969.

Beckett, Samuel. *Waiting for Godot*. New York: Grove Press,
1954.

Bennett, Alan. *Habeas Corpus*. London: Faber & Faber, 1973.

Berenson, Bernard. *Italian Painters of the Renaissance*, Vol. I.
London: Phaidon, 1968.

Berthold, Margot. *A History of World Theatre*, translated by
Edith Simmons. New York: Ungar, 1972.

Blofield, John. *The Tantric Mysticism of Tibet: A Practical
Guide*. New York: Dutton, 1970.

Bogoras, Waldemar. "Shamanistic Performance in the Inner Room," in *Reader in Comparative Religion*, edited by William A. Lessa and Evon G. Vogt (Evanston: Row, Peterson, 1958), pp. 414-420.

Bowers, Faubion. *Theatre in the East: A Survey of Asian Dance and Drama*. New York: Grove Press, 1960.

Brecht, Bertolt. *Parables for the Theatre*, translated by Eric Bentley and Maja Apelman. New York: Grove Press, 1948.

Brown, Roger. *Social Psychology*. New York: Free Press, 1965.

Brustein, Robert. *The Third Theatre*. New York: Knopf, 1969.

Buber, Martin. *The Origin and Meaning of Hasidism*, edited and translated by Maurice Friedman. New York: Horizon Press, 1960.

Carcopino, Jérôme. *Daily Life in Ancient Rome*, translated by E. O. Corimer. New York: Bantam, 1971.

Cassirer, Ernst. *Language and Myth*, translated by Suzanne K. Langer. New York: Dover, 1953.

Charles, Lucile Hoerr. "Drama in Shaman Exorcism," *Journal of American Folklore*, Vol. 66 (1953), pp. 95-122.

Chisman, Isabel, and Hester Emilie Raven-Hart. *Manners and Movements in Costume Plays*. London: Deane, n.d.

Chomsky, Noam. *Language and Mind*. New York: Harcourt, Brace & World, 1968.

Davis, Herbert, editor. *The Complete Plays of William Congreve*. Chicago: University of Chicago Press, 1967.

DeGeorge, Richard, and Fernande DeGeorge, editors. *The Structuralists: From Marx to Lévi-Strauss*. Garden City: Doubleday, 1972.

Douglas, Mary. *Natural Symbols: Explorations in Cosmology*. Harmondsworth: Penguin, 1973.

Dournes, Jacques. "Chamanisme à Mujat (Bornéo)," *Objets et Mondes*, Vol. XII (Spring 1972), pp. 23-44.

Duvignaud, Jean. *L'Acteur: Esquisse d'une sociologie du comédien*. Paris: Gallimard, 1965.

Eliade, Mircea. *Mephistopheles and the Androgyne: Studies in Religious Myth and Symbol*, translated by J. M. Cohen. New York: Sheed & Ward, 1965.

——. *Patterns in Comparative Religion*, translated by Rosemary Sheed. Cleveland: World, 1970.

——. *The Sacred and the Profane: The Nature of Religion*, translated by Willard R. Trask. New York: Harper, 1959.

——. *Shamanism: Archaic Techniques of Ecstasy*, translated by Willard R. Trask. Princeton: Princeton University Press, 1972.

Eliot, T. S. *The Cocktail Party*. New York: Harcourt, Brace & World, 1950.

Esslin, Martin. *The Peopled Wound: The Plays of Harold Pinter*. London: Methuen, 1970.

Firth, Raymond. "Ritual and Drama in Malay Spirit Mediumship," *Comparative Studies in Society and History*, Vol. IX (January 1967), pp. 190-207.

Freud, Sigmund. *Group Psychology and the Analysis of the Ego*, translated by James Strachey. New York: Bantam, 1971.

——. "A Neurosis of Demonical Possession in the Seventeenth Century," in *On Creativity and the Unconscious*. New York: Harper & Row, 1958.

——. *Psychopathology of Everyday Life*, translated by Alan Tyson. London: Benn, 1966.

——. *Totem and Taboo*, translated by James Strachey. New York: Norton, 1950.

——. "The Uncanny," in *On Creativity and the Unconscious*. New York: Harper & Row, 1958.

Gaster, Theodor H. "Myth and Story," *Numen*, Vol. I (1954), pp. 184-212.

Greimas, A. J., editor. *Essais de sémiotique poétique*. Paris: Larousse, 1972.

Grotowski, Jerzy. *Towards a Poor Theatre*. Holstebro, Denmark: Odin Teatrets Forlag, 1968.

Gurr, Andrew. *The Shakespearean Stage: 1574-1642*. Cambridge: Cambridge University Press, 1970.

Handke, Peter. *Calling for Help*, translated by Michael Roloff. *The Drama Review*, T 49 (Fall 1970), pp. 84-87.

Hardison, O. B. *Christian Rite and Christian Drama in the Middle Ages: Essays in the Origins and Early History of Modern Drama*. Baltimore: Johns Hopkins University Press, 1969.

Harrison, Jane Ellen. *Prolegomena to the Study of Greek Religion*. Cambridge: Cambridge University Press, 1903.

Hegel, Georg Wilhelm Friedrich. *Hegel: Texts and Commentary*, translated and edited by Walter Kaufmann. Garden City: Doubleday, 1966.

Heusch, Luc de. "Cultes de possession et religions initiatiques de salut en Afrique," in *Annales du Centre d'Etude des Religions* 2: *Religions du Salut*. Brussels: Université Libre de Bruxelles, 1962.

Hewitt, Bernard, editor. *The Renaissance Stage: Documents of Serlio, Sabbattini and Furtenbach*. Coral Gables: University of Miami Press, 1958.

Ibsen, Henrik. *Ghosts and Three Other Plays*, translated by Michael Meyer. Garden City: Doubleday, 1966.

Ionesco, Eugène. *Four Plays*, translated by Donald M. Allen. New York: Grove Press, 1958.

Jacobi, Jolande. *Complex/Archetype/Symbol in the Psychology of C. G. Jung*, translated by Ralph Manheim. Princeton: Princeton University Press, 1959.

Jonson, Ben. *The Complete Masques*, edited, with an introduction, by Stephen Orgel. New Haven: Yale University Press, 1969.

Jung, Carl, editor. *Man and His Symbols*. New York: Dell, 1968.

Kasanin, J. S., editor. *Language and Thought in Schizophrenia*. New York: Norton, 1964.

Kernodle, George R. *From Art to Theatre: Form and Convention in the Renaissance*. Chicago: University of Chicago Press, 1944.

Kirby, E. T., editor. *Total Theatre: A Critical Anthology.* New York: Dutton, 1969.

Kirby, Michael. *Futurist Performance.* (Playscripts translated by Victoria Nes Kirby.) New York: Dutton, 1971.

Laing, R. D. *The Divided Self: An Existential Study in Sanity and Madness.* Baltimore: Penguin, 1971.

Lambert, William W., and Wallace E. Lambert. *Social Psychology.* Englewood Cliffs: Prentice-Hall, 1964.

Leiris, Michel. *La Possession et ses aspects théâtraux chez les Ethiopiens de Gondar.* Paris: Plon, 1958.

Lewis, I. M. *Ecstatic Religion: An Anthropological Study of Spirit Possession and Shamanism.* Baltimore: Penguin, 1971.

Louis-Jean, Antonio. *La Crise de possession et la possession dramatique.* Ottawa: Leméac, 1970.

Luchins, A. S. "Social Influences on Perception of Complex Drawings," *The Journal of Social Psychology,* Vol. 21 (1945), pp. 257-273.

Magarshack, David. "Stanislavski," in *The Theory of the Modern Stage,* edited by Eric Bentley. Baltimore: Penguin, 1968.

Maruoka, Daiji, and Tatsuo Yoshikoshi. *Noh,* translated by Don Kenney. Osaka: Hoikusha, 1969.

May, Rollo. "Psychotherapy and the Daimonic," in *Myth, Dreams and Religion,* edited by Joseph Campbell. New York: Dutton, 1970.

Métraux, Alfred. "A Selection from *Voodoo in Haiti,*" in *Anthropology of Folk Religion,* edited by Charles Leslie. New York: Vintage, 1960.

Monfouga-Nicolas, Jacqueline. *Ambivalence et culte de possession: Contribution à l'étude du Bori hausa.* Paris: Anthropos, 1972.

Muir, Kenneth, and S. Schoenbaum, editors. *A New Companion to Shakespeare Studies.* Cambridge: Cambridge University Press, 1971.

Nagler, A. M. *A Source Book in Theatrical History.* New York: Dover, 1959.

Neilson, William Allan, and Charles Jarvis Hill, editors. *The Complete Plays and Poems of William Shakespeare.* Cambridge: Houghton Mifflin, 1942.

Nicoll, Allardyce. *Stuart Masques and the Renaissance Stage.* New York: Harcourt, Brace, 1938.

O'Casey, Sean. *Selected Plays of Sean O'Casey.* New York: Braziller, 1956.

Oesterreich, T. K. *Possession, Demonical and Other.* London: Kegan Paul, 1930.

Osgood, Charles E., and Thomas A. Sebeok. *Psycholinguistics: A Survey of Theory and Research.* Bloomington: Indiana University Press, 1965.

Pasolli, Robert. *A Book on the Open Theatre.* Indianapolis: Bobbs-Merrill, 1970.

Pinter, Harold. *The Caretaker and The Dumb Waiter.* New York: Grove Press, 1965.

Pirandello, Luigi. *Naked Masks: Five Plays*, edited by Eric Bentley. New York: Dutton, 1958.

Pound, Ezra, and Ernest Fenellosa. *The Classic Noh Theatre of Japan.* New York: New Directions, 1959. [Includes an Introduction by William Butler Yeats, pp. 151-163.]

Racamier, P. C. "Hystérie et théâtre," *L'Evolution Psychiatrique,* Vol. II (1952), pp. 257-291.

Reinhardt, Max. "Of Actors," *The Yale Review* (New Series), Vol. 18 (1928-29), pp. 31-38.

Rilke, Rainer Marie. *Duino Elegies*, translated by J. B. Leishman and Stephen Spender. New York: Norton, 1967.

Róheim, Géza. *The Gates of the Dream.* New York: International Universities Press, 1970.

Rouch, Jean. *La Religion et la magie songhay.* Paris: Presses Universitaires de France, 1960.

Sargant, William. *The Mind Possessed: A Physiology of Possession, Mysticism and Faith Healing.* London: Heineman, 1973.

Schechner, Richard. *Public Domain: Essays on the Theatre.* Indianapolis: Bobbs-Merrill, 1969.

Séchehaye, Marguérite, editor. *Autobiography of a Schizophrenic Girl.* New York: New American Library, 1970.

Slobin, Dan I. *Psycholinguistics.* Glenview: Scott, Foresman, 1971.

Sokel, Walter H., editor. *An Anthology of German Expressionist Drama.* Garden City: Doubleday, 1963.

Southern, Richard. *The Seven Ages of the Theatre.* New York: Hill & Wang, 1963.

Spolin, Viola. *Improvisation for the Theatre: A Handbook of Teaching and Directing Techniques.* Evanston: Northwestern University Press, 1969.

Stanislavski, Constantin. *An Actor Prepares,* translated by Elizabeth Reynolds Hapgood. New York: Theatre Arts, 1961.

——. *Building a Character,* translated by Elizabeth Reynolds Hapgood. New York: Theatre Arts, 1949.

——. *Creating a Role,* translated by Elizabeth Reynolds Hapgood. New York: Theatre Arts, 1961.

Synge, John Millington. *The Playboy of the Western World and Riders to the Sea.* Northbrook: AHM, 1966.

Tairov, Alexander. *Notes of a Director,* translated, with an introduction, by William Kuhlke. Coral Gables: University of Miami Press, 1969.

Wilson, F. A. C. *W. B. Yeats and Tradition.* London: Gollancz, 1961.

——. *Yeats's Iconography.* London: Gollancz, 1960.

Wittgenstein, Ludwig. *The Blue and Brown Books.* New York: Harper & Row, 1965.

——. *Tractatus Logico-Philosophicus.* London: Routledge & Kegan Paul, 1960.

Yale/Theatre, Vol. 2 (Spring 1969): "The Living Theatre."

Yeats, William Butler. *The Collected Plays of W. B. Yeats.* New York: Macmillan, 1953.